If You Give
A Damn About
L I F E

HAROLD FREEMAN
Preface by Bernard T. Feld

DODD   Y

New York

To The Hibakusha

A short version
of this book was published under
the title *This Is The Way The World
Will End This is the Way You Will
End Unless* . . . in 1982 by Schenkman
Publishing Company, Cambridge, Massachusetts and
in 1983 by Hurtig Publishers, Edmonton, Canada.

Published by Dodd, Mead & Company, Inc.
79 Madison Avenue, New York, N.Y. 10016
Distributed in Canada by
McClelland and Stewart Limited, Toronto
Manufactured in the United States of America
Designed by Nancy Dale Muldoon
First Edition

Library of Congress Cataloging in Publication Data

Freeman, Harold.
    If you give a damn about life.

    Includes index.
    1. Nuclear warfare—Moral and ethical aspects.
I. Title.
U263.F72   1985   355'.0217   84-21212
ISBN 0-396-08615-2 (pbk.)

They made a desert and they called it peace.

Tacitus

Against a great evil, a small remedy does not produce a small result; it produces no result at all.

John Stuart Mill

O Blessed Lady, look down graciously upon the fields and pastures of this land. Make our homes sanctuaries of Christ as was thy home. Make our fields fertile and abundant in the harvest. Help us to more fully understand the dignity of our toil and the merit it acquires when offered through thee to thy Divine Son, Jesus Christ. Amen.

Inscription on a churchyard shrine in the town of St. Francis, Texas, where all American nuclear bombs reach final assembly

Prevention of nuclear war is not only the great issue of our time, but the greatest issue of all time.

Senator Edward Kennedy

Contents

Preface

To the growing numbers of those of us who are worried about the future of *Homo sapiens*, these are critical times. On the one hand, the stockpiles of nuclear bombs—already enough to destroy all the antagonists at least ten times over—continue to multiply at an obscene rate, while the six nations that have already publicly demonstrated their nuclear weapons capabilities are being joined—privately or publicly—by others at a rate that threatens to triple their number by the end of this decade. On the other hand, public awareness of their dangers—together with an unwillingness to continue to suffer the nuclear status quo—already visibly manifested in Western Europe, is rapidly spreading in the United States and, indeed, in Eastern Europe as well, including the heretofore placid citizenry of the Soviet Union.

Indeed, we appear to be witnessing the development of a critical race between the nuclear hardliners and an aroused public or, to put it in perhaps overdramatic terms, between the quick and the dead. But in this case, the dead are refusing to lie down.

It may well be, as Harold Freeman contends, that only an aroused public, taking to the streets, can turn the tide against nuclear destruction. But I would also contend that all the evidence is not yet in that would convince me that we may not yet still be able to triumph via the ballot box. Noting the passing of public referendums, and the rapid spreading of this idea throughout the rest of the nation, an aroused citizenry could still force its "representatives" to do its bidding on the issues of the nuclear freeze, a revival of SALT—let them call it START—and, yes, even eventually toward official acceptance of the "no-first-use" concept.

But an aroused public opinion must be fueled with the facts—in a form that is understandable and readily accessible. To this end, this essay can serve an invaluable purpose coming, as it does, at a critical time, and lucid and accurate as it is. I would hope that, with Freeman's help, the message will soon be taken up by many more voices.

Bernard T. Feld
Editor, *Bulletin of the Atomic Scientists*

ONE
One Bomb

A twenty-year-old man received extensive third-degree burns when the gasoline tank of his car exploded. He was taken to Massachusetts General Hospital, the only hospital in Boston with a major-burn care unit. Over the period of his hospitalization he received 281 units of fresh-frozen plasma, 147 units of fresh-frozen red blood cells, 37 units of platelets, and 36 units of albumin. He underwent six operations, during which 85% of his body surface was covered with skin grafts. He was kept on artificial respiration because his lungs had been scorched out. Treating him stretched the resources of the burn care unit to the limit.

On the thirty-third day he died.

Boston

There will one day spring from the brain of science a machine or force so fearful in its potentialities, so absolutely terrifying that even man, the fighter, who will dare torture and death in order to inflict torture and death, will be appalled and so abandon war altogether.

Thomas Edison

Now imagine that one twenty-megaton* nuclear bomb is dropped on Boston. Of those who survive, 1,000,000 will receive second- or

---

*One megaton is an explosive yield equivalent to one million metric tons of TNT; one kiloton to one thousand metric tons of TNT.

third-degree burns from ignited clothing. As at Hiroshima, much of their skin will hang in shreds. For them there will be no plasma, no skin grafts. There will be no hospitals. Most of them will die painfully; morphine will not reach them.

In the United States there are three major-burn care units with a total of one hundred beds.* They are meant primarily for children. Construction and operation were financed by the Shriners. Costs were so high that no more units could be built. Between $200,000 and $400,000 is needed to treat *one* severe burn case. Treatment may include up to fifty operative procedures, anesthesia every other day, infection-proof enclosures, and constant attention. At most a major-burn care unit can handle three fresh severe cases at once.

Dr. John Constable of Massachusetts General Hospital writes that even if all medical facilities in the United States, as well as all transport, can be preserved, thermal injuries in one large city from even a one-megaton nuclear bomb "will completely overwhelm what we consider to be one of the most lavish and well-developed medical facilities in the world." In the face of nuclear explosions, which include hospitals and transport in the destruction, "the medical facilities of the nation would choke totally on even a fraction of the resulting burn casualties alone."

From experience in wartime London, International Physicians for the Prevention of Nuclear War estimate that acute treatment of 34,000 serious burn cases would require 170,000 health professionals and 8,000 tons of medical supplies. When the bomb falls there will be neither.

Burned survivors will be only a part of the picture. Within a radius of four miles of a twenty-megaton bomb burst, Greater Boston will literally disappear. It will be replaced by rubble. More than 750,000

---

*In nuclear warfare we will generally be dealing with second- and third-degree burns— the latter always, the former often, life-threatening. Moreover, the combination of radiation and even first-degree burns may produce pain beyond human endurance. The American Burn Association lists 185 hospitals in the United States, including 145 with special burn units, able to house a total of 1,700 patients. But *severe* burns can be treated in considerably fewer hospitals. Example: Although the ABA lists 18 burn hospitals in California in the special category, two young Wyoming brothers, Jamie and Glen Selby, burned over 97% of their bodies, had, after heroic efforts at Memorial Hospital of Natrona County, Wyoming, and Children's Hospital in Denver, to be flown by private jet to the Shriners Burn Institute at Massachusetts General in Boston (40 beds), one of the three burn centers in this country equipped to handle severe cases; in this extreme case, the *only* hospital. The other two are in Galveston (30 beds) and Cincinnati (30 beds). One hundred major-burn beds remains a fair (and pathetic) estimate.

will die at once, from concussion, heat, or fire. Many will be vaporized. Fire-wind storms resembling winter blizzards will originate in a fireball hotter than the sun, and will sweep a radius of twenty miles. Within that radius 2,200,000 will die. Another 500,000 will be disabled and in shock. Their injuries will include deep chest wounds, ruptured internal organs, compound fractures, radiation sickness, and blindness. Anyone who looks at the fireball from a distance of forty miles or less will likely be blinded.

Epidemic disease, carried by radiation-resistant flies and mosquitoes and by hunger-crazed animals, will end the suffering of more than 25% of the weakened survivors. In the judgment of several authorities, such diseases as polio, dysentery, typhoid fever, and cholera will reappear in force.

Of the dead, 300,000 will neither be vaporized nor incinerated. The Pentagon has asked the National Funeral Directors Association of the United States to prepare to handle mass burials; the president of the Association has asked for a training course in embalming radioactive corpses. One thing is certain. Unburied, buried, incinerated, or vaporized, the dead will continue to be radioactive—forever.

Of Greater Boston's 6,500 doctors, 5,600 will be incapacitated or dead. That will leave 900 to treat the injured. Dr. Howard Hiatt, former Dean of the Harvard School of Public Health, writes:

The ratio of injured persons to physicians thus would exceed 1,700 to 1. If a physician spent an average of only fifteen minutes with each injured person and worked sixteen hours each day . . . it would take from sixteen to twenty-six days for each casualty to be seen once.

Doctors will have to treat the maimed where they lie, in the radioactive rubble, and with little more than bare hands. There will be no anesthesia, no bandages, few drugs.* Consider blood alone. Close to 10,000,000 units would be needed. On one recent day the total blood inventory of the entire northeast region of the American Red Cross was

---

*When asked how he would allocate federal money in the period immediately following the bomb, one doctor replied, "Use it all on morphine." The Federal Emergency Management Agency may not be in total disagreement with this view. FEMA has stockpiled 72,000 pounds (40,000 pounds of powdered morphine sulfate and 32,000 pounds of raw gum opium—morphine is a derivative of opium) for critical civilian use. After a "reanalysis of nuclear requirements," FEMA requested 59,000 additional pounds; the Reagan administration has delayed adding to the stockpile, seeking to avoid a war-ready image.

11,000 units. Alfred Gellhorn and Penny Janeway, of the Harvard School of Public Health write:

In the event of a nuclear attack upon one medium-sized city, the entire United States blood supply for a year could be required within the first 24 hours.

Even if every injured person in the city could miraculously be lifted out of the rubble by helicopter, all the hospitals in the United States would be insufficient in resources to handle them. In fact, the majority of the injured—those suffering from severe radiation—might not even be admitted to a hospital. Here are instructions from the British Civil Defense Manual:

Hospitals should accept only those casualties who would be likely to be alive after seven days with a fair chance of eventual recovery.*. . . People suffering from radiation sickness only should not be admitted. There is no specific treatment for radiation injury. . . . Treatment of a person exposed to heavy radiation would probably include bone marrow transplants, blood transfusions, and continuous use of antibiotics. None would likely be available.

Death by early radiation could require a month. Here is one description of the process:

The first symptoms of radiation poisoning are headache, nausea, dizziness and frequent vomiting, then acute diarrhea and fatigue. This lasts several days and is followed by apparent recovery, but two or three weeks later the symptoms return together with internal hemorrhaging. Breathing becomes difficult, hair falls out, sores appear under and on the skin; there is fever, total fatigue, and finally death.

The Neutron Bomb

But death by radiation may not always be that easy. Consider the neutron bomb, now operational in the United States,† and now in the early construction stage in (socialist) France. It is easily built. It causes death by radiation (neutrons and gamma rays), not by heat or blast. Representative

---

*At an early stage, it is not possible to separate mild and severe cases of radiation sickness. Reliable tests are not available, and the victims look and behave alike.

†In April 1978, President Carter deferred production of the neutron bomb. In August 1981, President Reagan ordered full-scale production. Publicly unnoticed, neutron bombs are now being produced and stored in the United States.

Barbara Mikulski of Maryland has reported her conversation with Dr. Edward Buddemeyer, a nuclear physicist at the University of Maryland:

He [Buddemeyer] said that the neutron bomb explodes and blows so many holes in your nerve cells that your brain ceases to function. If it does not, you will collapse and you will lose control of your body functions. You will die within minutes or perhaps hours, and while you are lying there waiting for death to call, you will lie in your own wastes, in your own feces, with rapid convulsions and shaking.

The second cause of death, if you are a little further away, will come from something called the GI syndrome. At first you will retch and vomit. Then the nausea will pass, but you will not feel like eating because the cells in your digestive tract, extending from your mouth down through your throat and down into your stomach, will continue to divide and die, and by that time your digestive tract will become an open sore.

Your heart will weaken, your kidneys will fail, your fever will climb and you are going to hallucinate. As you lie there dying, the very insides of your body will be rotting.

The third way to die will be from the blood syndrome. If you are lucky, you will die of anemia. This will be the more peaceful option, because the neutron will attack the blood cells so they will no longer be able to reproduce. If anemia does not claim a victim on the periphery of a neutron bomb blast, death will be prolonged and agonizing. A mere hangnail will become a green ulcer, since disease defense mechanisms will be destroyed by the neutron radiation. Your gums will bleed and your mouth will hemorrhage. Microbes will grow in your lungs and they will lose their elasticity. Fluid will begin to gather and, in effect, your own lungs will become a swamp within your body.

As you gasp and struggle for breath, your liver will fail and your skin will turn yellow. You will then perhaps die or drown from your own contaminated body fluids contained in your lungs and your liver. This will take four to five weeks, while you are lying there.

Two notes on the neutron bomb:

1. *The* (Manchester) *Guardian* reports that the United States Navy has already experimented with high doses (2,500 to 20,000 rems*) of neutron-gamma radiation. Within 132 hours monkeys in the experiments died very painful deaths. Much of the experimentation took place at the Armed Forces Radiobiology Research Institute at Bethesda, Maryland.

---

*A rem is a unit of radiation dosage used in connection with human exposure. The American official safe absorption rate for humans is five rems per year; in the judgment of some scientists, that rate is too high.

2. Former Secretary of State Alexander Haig remarks that the "great emotional complaints" that have arisen over this weapon are "ludicrous."
Secretary of Defense Caspar Weinberger says, "The opportunity that this
weapon gives to strengthening theater nuclear forces is one that we very
probably want to make use of."

New York City

We cannot defend, we can only kill.

Rear Admiral Gene LaRocque,
United States Navy (ret.)

Consider a one-megaton bomb. It equals 77 Hiroshima bombs. "It
would take a train 300 miles long to transport the equivalent dynamite,"
writes Dr. Kosta Tsipis of MIT. One such bomb could vaporize ten
million tons of ice. One such bomb equals half of the total destructive
power of *all* bombs used by the Western Allies in Europe during *all* of
World War II. Nuclear bombs of this size are currently stockpiled by
the thousands in the United States and the Soviet Union.

At a conference of physicists and doctors, a consensus was reached
on the impact on New York City of the detonation, *above* ground level,
of such a bomb.

The fireball, hotter than the sun, will be about 1 1/2 miles in diameter. Centering on the explosion (ground zero), the firestorm will
cover about 100 square miles, destroying most of whatever and whomever stands on that area. Fatal third-degree burns are likely for those
within a radius of eight miles of burst, second-degree burns will be
common out to a radius of 9.5 miles (284 square miles). Shelters in
the larger area will become ovens, incinerating their occupants.

The blast wave will reduce almost all buildings within a radius of
three miles (28 square miles) to rubble. In greater detail, with an explosion 6,000 feet above ground:

Radius	Wind Velocity	Blast Damage
2 miles	500 miles per hour	all buildings demolished
3 miles	300 miles per hour	almost all buildings demolished
4 miles	160 miles per hour	heavy damage
7 miles	60 miles per hour	moderate damage

Skyscrapers will topple. It is unlikely that a single metropolitan hospital will remain standing. New York City will be replaced by acres of highly radioactive rubble. There will be no communication, no transport, few medicines, no edible food, no drinkable water.

In New York City, 1,700,000–2,000,000 will die quickly. Of that number, 750,000–1,000,000 will die within eleven seconds, many of them vaporized; 2,800,000–3,400,000 will be seriously injured. The lower figures are by the United States Arms Control and Disarmament Agency; the higher figures, by Dr. H. Jack Geiger, assume a *weekday* bombing. Injuries will include crushed chest, abdomen and limbs, skull fracture, spinal cord injury, multiple lacerations, hemorrhaging, shock, radiation sickness, and burns.

Radioactive fallout will be one thousand times greater than the fallout of the worst conceivable nuclear power reactor accident. It will likely blanket 1,000 square miles. All unprotected people (who will have survived heat, fire and blast) within an area of 600 square miles will likely die from radioactive fallout, with substantial risk of death extending over an additional 1,000 square miles. Farther out, specific areas of death and injury will depend on prevailing winds. A wind as light as twenty miles per hour will carry lethal fallout hundreds of miles from burst. Death will take longer, but it will arrive via such diseases as leukemia (particularly for children), ulceration of the intestines, cancer of the lungs, thyroid, breast, and intestine, and bone cancer. For longer-term survivors there will be other consequences—genetic damage, psychological trauma of every description, mental retardation, concentration of plutonium in testicles and ovaries (for 50,000 years), and abnormalities in new births. Khrushchev was right; the living will envy the dead.

Some species will survive, notably cockroaches. They will be blind but they will continue to reproduce.

Consider one *twenty-megaton* nuclear bomb, airburst over New York City. From 7,700,000–9,200,000 will die; 3,900,000–4,600,000 will be seriously injured. Once again, the lower figures are by the Arms Control and Disarmament Agency, the higher figures by Dr. Geiger. Second- and third-degree burns will be common out to twenty-eight miles from ground zero (2,463 square miles). Burn victims will number close to one thousand times the capacity of all burn centers in the United States. Out to a radius of twelve miles, the area will be largely rubble.

7

Now consider one twenty-megaton nuclear bomb, groundburst. Some 2,200,000–3,000,000 will die, most from silent heat flash. Of these, many will be vaporized. Out to ten miles, 50% of the population will die and 40% will be injured. Out to twenty miles, 50% will die or be injured. Again, those facing the explosion from forty miles or less will likely suffer blindness from retinal burn.

The crater will be one and a half miles in diameter; within a radius of four miles, rubble only. Within a radius of fifteen miles, all frame structures will be demolished.

The fireball will be six miles in diameter, with a core temperature of 20–30 million degrees Fahrenheit. Initial winds may be as high as 1,000 miles per hour; along with blast, the raging firestorm will be the major early killer. Twelve hundred square miles of coalesced random fires will supplement the firestorm.

Is there any defense? No. Admiral LaRocque, now director of the Center for Defense Information, writes that annihilation could come in

fifteen minutes from the submarines sitting off the coast right now with nuclear weapons aimed at Boston and New York. There is no defense against Soviet missiles, absolutely none.*

Omaha

A probable target is the Strategic Air Command, fifteen miles from Omaha. The Command is the control center for all American strategic nuclear forces; the long list of targets in the Soviet Union is housed there. Here is Dr. Geiger's description of the likely effect on the Command of the explosion of a fifteen-megaton nuclear bomb:

In the seconds following detonation, the bomb would create a huge fireball with temperatures of twenty to thirty million degrees Fahrenheit. Anyone even

---

*Sixty-two (invulnerable) Soviet submarines carry 930 missiles armed with 2,100 nuclear weapons. Relatively few of these submarines are at sea. Of the 2,100 nuclear weapons, 300 are targeted day and night on the United States.

Thirty-six (invulnerable) American submarines (5 Trident, 31 Poseidon) carry 616 missiles armed with 5,540 nuclear weapons. Sixty percent of American submarines are at sea. Of the 5,540 nuclear weapons, 3,000 are targeted day and night on the Soviet Union.

glancing at the fireball—from as far away as thirty-five miles—would be blinded by retinal burning. Tens of thousands of people on the side of Omaha closest to the SAC base would suffer third-degree burns.

The shock wave created by the explosion would cause skull fractures, ruptured lungs, and crushing injuries to the chest. There would be broken backs, deep lacerations from flying debris, and massive hemorrhaging. Even at eleven or twelve miles from ground zero, the overpressure would be great enough to turn an ordinary window into a lethal weapon as thousands of pieces of glass exploded at one hundred miles per hour.

These injuries do not include the many who would be killed by random spontaneous fires fueled by gasoline stations, natural gas lines, and oil storage tanks. These fires could coalesce into a firestorm burning Omaha and its surroundings for six to eight hours. With temperatures as high as 1,600 degrees Fahrenheit, many in shelters would be dry roasted, as in a crematorium. Others would be asphyxiated as the fire sucked the oxygen out of their shelters.

Chicago

Another likely target, another scenario, a different set of estimates. One twenty-megaton nuclear bomb explodes just above ground level, at the corner of LaSalle and Adams. In less than one millionth of a second the temperature rises to 150,000,000 degrees Fahrenheit, four times the temperature of the center of the sun. A roar follows but no one is alive to hear it.

Chicago has disappeared. The crater is 600 feet deep, one and a half miles in diameter. Within a five-mile radius, skyscrapers, apartment buildings, roads, bridges, trains, subways, planes, hospitals, ambulances, automobiles, gas mains, trees, earth, animals, people—all have vanished. For inner-city people it was instant, painless death, occurring before the firestorm or the shock wave began to move out.

The fireball is brighter than five thousand suns. The firestorm roars out in all directions, absorbing all available oxygen, thereby suffocating or incinerating all the living in its path. Before it burns out it will devastate 1,400,000 acres and most of the people on them.

The firestorm is followed by the shock wave, the latter at close to the speed of sound. Then the mushroom cloud, reaching twenty miles in height, and the beginning of lethal radioactive fallout. If the prevailing wind is from the west, and it usually is, 50% of the residents of Kalamazoo, one hundred miles away, will be dead in fifteen hours; 100% will be dead in twenty-four hours. Detroit is 230 miles east of

Chicago and will survive longer; within three weeks 50% of its population will die; within one year 100% will be dead. But, as the authors of this scenario note, this last calculation is probably irrelevant; Detroit will have already been hit. *

For a twenty-megaton nuclear bomb an independent estimate has been made for Chicago. Briefly, (1) all property within 4 miles of burst reduced to rubble, (2) immediate death to all persons within 10 miles of burst, (3) average life expectancy for those 10 to 20 miles away will be less than four minutes, (4) a 10% survival rate for those 20 to 30 miles away, (5) within 150 miles of Chicago, all in the wind path will eventually die of radiation; within 300 miles, up to 90% will die.

Add in the emotional trauma which accompanies these massive numbers. Along with knowing that nameless millions are suffering horrors, survivors will have to live with doubts about family and friends, nearby and further away. What about the daughter visiting friends? The husband at work? If Chicago is bombed, what is happening to parents hundreds of miles away but in the path of radiation?

San Francisco

0.0 to 1.5 Miles

A one-megaton bomb is exploded near ground level at City Hall. Almost all would be killed. The Civic Center, the Opera House and most of nearby elderly housing would disappear in a crater twenty stories deep. Radioactive soil would be thrown thousands of feet into the air. The explosion would create winds up to 500 miles per hour. Nothing recognizable would remain from the Old Mint on Mission to St. Mary's Cathedral and Japantown. Little of significance would remain standing from the Mission and Potrero districts on the south, to Russian Hill on the north, from the Panhandle on the west to the financial district and Chinatown on the east. This destruction of buildings and people would occur in seconds.

---

*For a detailed account of devastation if Detroit (or Leningrad) is hit by a one-megaton or a twenty-five-megaton bomb, see *The Effects of Nuclear War* by the Office of Technological Assessment of the United States Congress, or the summary and analysis of the grim account in the book *Nukespeak*. One twenty-five-megaton nuclear bomb has considerably greater destructive power than the 1906 earthquake which destroyed San Francisco.

Heat from the explosion and instant burning of clothing would cause third-degree flash burns for most people in this area, killing at least 50% of them. Brick and wood frame buildings would be destroyed. Fanned by 160-mile-per-hour winds, vast firestorms would follow the intense heat. Thousands would die from lack of oxygen. Underground shelters, if there were any, would become ovens. Pressure from the blast would convert shattered glass into missiles traveling at over 100 miles per hour. Transportation would be destroyed or made useless. Emergency medical equipment and supplies would be destroyed.

5.0 Miles and Beyond

Intense light from the explosion could cause retinal damage and even blindness to those who face the explosion. Among survivors, many would be deaf, a consequence of ruptured eardrums. Up to hundreds of miles away, with specification depending on wind direction and other factors, radiation would kill thousands; radiation would be spread by tons of settling contaminated soil, as well as by floating or drifting debris. For any who survive these threats to life, recovery will be long and painful, likely accompanied by permanent disability.

Montreal

We apply to Montreal estimates of loss of life and property recently published by Physicians for Social Responsibility.

A twenty-megaton nuclear bomb is exploded at ground level on Dominion Square. At point of burst, temperatures will reach 20 million to 30 million degrees Fahrenheit. In downtown Montreal all things and all living beings will be vaporized.

The fireball will be nearly 3 miles in radius. Within 6 miles of the epicenter, roughly out to St.-Leonard-de-Port-Maurice to the north, Bronx Park to the south, and St.-Laurent to the west, all persons will be killed by silent heat flash; the flash will travel at the speed of light. Winds of 225 miles per hour and a supersonic shock wave will collapse buildings, including all hospitals.

Within a 10-mile radius, out to Ville de Laval to the northwest, a combination of blast wave, 100-mile-per-hour winds, and fire will leave 50% of the population dead and 40% injured; many of the injured will be burned. At 20 miles from the epicenter, that is, as far out as St.-

Jean to the southeast, 50% of the population will either be killed or injured by blast pressure or by direct thermal radiation.

A 20-mile-per-hour wind will carry radioactive fallout 150 miles from the burst. All exposed persons in the wind path will probably acquire lethal doses of radiation in twenty-four hours, with death likely in one to two weeks.

Death in the Suburbs

A one-megaton nuclear bomb is detonated at ground level* in Waltham, Massachusetts, an important industrial suburb of Boston. Analysis is by the Council for a Livable World.

Damage from blast

Within a ½ mile radius, no survivors; all buildings destroyed.

Within a 2½ mile radius, few survivors; all buildings gutted or destroyed.

Within a 4¼ mile radius, flying debris will wound many; severe damage to all houses.

Damage from heat

The firestorm will reach everything and everyone within a radius of 10½ miles; winds at 100 miles per hour.

Within a radius of 7⅓ miles, all persons exposed to the initial flash will suffer third-degree burns. Survival chances minimal. Flash area includes much of Boston.

Within a radius of 10½ miles, all exposed persons will suffer second-degree burns. All wood, cloth, and dry leaves will catch fire.

Damage from radioactive fallout

3,000 rem: All receiving this dosage will die within hours. Area: 1½ miles west of ground zero extending in an arc 2½ miles to the north and the same distance to the south, and then to the northeast and southeast. †Includes Boston, Cambridge, and numerous major inner suburbs.

---

*If a one-megaton bomb is detonated at a nuclear reactor site, the enemy gets a bonus. 50,000 square miles become inaccessible for at least a year; plus, there are additional radiation deaths.

†The prevailing west-east wind pattern results in C-shaped zones of radioactive fallout.

1,000 rem: All receiving this dosage will die within one or two weeks. Area: 3 miles west of ground zero extending in an arc 5 miles to the north and the same distance to the south, and then to the northeast and southeast. Includes heavily populated Malden, Medford, Arlington, Newton, and Dorchester.

100 rem: About 10% of the population receiving this dosage, particularly children, the elderly and the infirm, will die within a few weeks. The remainder will suffer from radiation illness—vomiting, loss of hair, infection—and may later develop leukemia and other cancers; also genetic damage. Area: five miles west of ground zero extending in an arc about six miles to the north and the same distance to the south, and then to the northeast and southeast. Includes heavily populated Saugus, Melrose, Winchester, Weston, Milton, and Quincy.

Washington and Moscow

A final example: Each capital is hit by a (modest) one-megaton groundburst nuclear bomb. The effects are based on calculations published by Ruth Leger Sivard in her invaluable annual report, *World Military and Social Expenditures 1982*.

Epicenter: The bomb (77 times the power of the Hiroshima bomb) creates a crater 300 feet deep and 1,200 feet in diameter. All life and structures are pulverized.

0–0.6 mile: People, vehicles, buildings, and thousands of tons of earth are swept into a luminous fireball, with temperatures hotter than the sun. The fireball, one mile wide and rising to a height of more than 6 miles, incinerates all life below in less than 10 seconds.

0.6–2 miles: The flash from the explosion sweeps outward from the epicenter at the speed of light. A shock wave of compressed air creates overpressures from 100 pounds per square inch (psi) at 0.6 mile to 9 psi at 2 miles. Structures as well as people are crushed. Lethal radiation covers the area. Virtually everyone dies immediately.

2–3 miles: Trees, clothing, and combustible materials ignite spontaneously. Winds exceed one hundred miles per hour. Overpressures blow out walls of even the largest buildings. Fifty percent of the people die immediately; many of the rest die more slowly from radioactive poisoning, burns, broken bodies, and deeply imbedded fragments of glass.

3–5 miles:	Frame buildings are blown out or leveled. Fuel storage tanks explode. Intense heat causes third-degree burns to all exposed skin. A firestorm is highly probable; if it occurs, it will suck oxygen out of underground stations, asphyxiating the occupants. Shelters become ovens. Close to fifty percent of the people die immediately; if there is a firestorm, very few survive the day.
5–10 miles:	The shock wave, traveling one mile in five seconds, reaches the Capital Beltway and Moscow Ring Road 40 seconds after the blast. People in exposed locations suffer second-degree burns. The scorched area covers 200 square miles. Radioactive fallout creates an immediately lethal zone of 400 square miles, causing death through massive damage to the central nervous system and bone marrow.

Moving downwind in a huge plume, radioactive fallout also contaminates up to 20,000 square miles.

A Single Bomb, A Crippled Nation

It is possible for a *single* ten- or fifteen- or twenty-megaton nuclear bomb to cripple the entire nation. Exploded 300 miles above the center of the United States, the electromagnetic energy released by the bomb could put 50,000 volts into every metal antenna. Electric power, as well as telephone, television, and radio networks, will be disrupted. Public and private business will find it difficult to function. Agencies operating special computerized communication networks might be unable to continue at all. Such agencies include the Social Security Administration, the Federal Reserve banking system, the Internal Revenue Service, and the Federal Bureau of Investigation.

Hiroshima

Now I am become death, the destroyer of worlds.

J. Robert Oppenheimer,
from the *Bhagavad Gita*

This is the greatest thing in history.

President Harry Truman

. . . we must remember that it has been we Americans who, at almost every step of the road, have taken the lead

14

*in the development of this sort of weaponry. It was we
who first produced and tested such a device; we who were
the first to raise its destructiveness to a new level with the
hydrogen bomb; we who introduced the multiple warhead;
we who have declined every proposal for the renunciation
of the principle of "first use"; and we alone, so help us
God, who have used the weapon in anger against others,
and against tens of thousands of helpless non-combatants
at that.*

George Kennan,
on accepting the Einstein Peace Award, May 1981

For those who want facts, not conjectures, there are a few. Twice in history have atomic bombs been used in combat, both times by the United States. The first fell on Hiroshima,* the second on Nagasaki. The bombs were small, at Hiroshima uranium-fueled and only thirteen kiloton, at Nagasaki plutonium-fueled and twenty-two kiloton. Yet the results are memorable.

In Hiroshima, at the point of explosion about 2,000 feet above ground, the temperature reached several million degrees Fahrenheit in one-millionth of a second. The firestorm was 1½ miles in circumference; it raged for four hours. The temperature at the center of the fireball is estimated at 300,000 degrees Fahrenheit. Many persons were vaporized; the shadows of some of them remain to this day. Moving at the speed of sound, at about 760 miles per hour, the shock wave covered an area of three square miles in seconds, then reversed itself; of the city's 76,000 buildings, 90% were destroyed, along with most of their occupants. After the mushroom cloud formed, an oily, highly radioactive "black rain" fell for thirty to sixty minutes, bringing early death to thousands outside the firestorm and the shock wave. Out of a resident population of 245,000, over 110,000 were killed. Another 80,000 were injured, 30,000 seriously.

One hundred and twenty-six of 1,780 nurses and fewer than 30 of 150 doctors were able to treat the injured. One hospital (Red Cross)

---

*American leadership considered the idea of dropping the first atomic bomb on an uninhabited forest near Tokyo, to demonstrate to the Japanese its power. But Hiroshima was finally chosen.

survived. From John Hersey's *Hiroshima*, here is an account of the only uninjured doctor at Red Cross:

Dr. Sasaki worked without method, taking those who were nearest him first, and he noticed soon that the corridor seemed to be getting more and more crowded. Mixed in with the abrasions and lacerations which most people in the hospital had suffered, he began to find dreadful burns. He realized that casualties were pouring in from outdoors. There were so many that he began to pass up the lightly wounded; he decided that all he could hope to do was to stop people from bleeding to death. Before long, patients lay and crouched on the floors of the wards and the laboratories and all other rooms, and in the corridors, and on the stairs, and in the front hall, and under the porte cochere, and on the stone front steps, and in the driveway and courtyard, and for blocks each way in the streets outside. Wounded people supported maimed people; disfigured families leaned together. Many people were vomiting. A tremendous number of schoolgirls—some of those who had been taken from their classrooms to work outdoors, clearing fire lanes—crept into the hospital. . . . The people in the suffocating crowd inside the hospital wept and cried, for Dr. Sasaki to hear, "*Sensai!* Doctor!" and the less seriously wounded came and pulled at his sleeve and begged him to go to the aid of the worse wounded. Tugged here and there in his stockinged feet, bewildered by the numbers, staggered by so much raw flesh, Dr. Sasaki lost all sense of profession and stopped working as a skillful surgeon and a sympathetic man; he became an automaton, mechanically wiping, daubing, winding, wiping, daubing, winding.

Surviving children were particularly vulnerable. Via contaminated milk, radioactivity penetrated their bones and remained stored there, sooner or later likely to produce leukemia. Cirrhosis of the liver was common. Another radioactive by-product, Iodine 131, led to cancer of the thyroid as well as to mongolism.

In the weeks, months, and years that followed, deaths continued. Leukemia, a variety of tumors, cataracts, and cancers, diffuse hemorrhage, infection, and uncontrollable vomiting were soon commonplace. Grotesque skin excrescenses appeared, as well as mental retardation, deafness, and children born with small heads. In the five years following the bomb, as many died in Hiroshima from cancer via radiation as were killed on that fateful morning.* Thirty-five years after the explosion, 2,500 still die annually from the bomb's cumulative radiation. Among

---

*8:15 A.M., August 6, 1945.

current causes of death are malignant lymphoma, leukemia, thyroid cancer, lung and breast cancer, and salivary gland tumors.

Stories told by survivors have been collected. A child's face full of window glass splinters, a woman without a jaw wandering amid the rubble, a child burned black with frozen arms reaching toward the sky, a live horse on fire, a baby trying to nurse its dead mother, the fingers of a human hand burning with a blue flame.

Here are brief excerpts from five of the quieter accounts:

1. A Hiroshima woman:
   I was shocked by the feeling that the skin of my face had come off. Then, the hands and arms, too. . . . All the skin of my right hand came off and hung down grotesquely. . . . Hundreds of people were squirming in the stream. Their faces were swollen and gray, their hair was standing up. Holding their hands high, groaning, people were rushing to the river.

2. A Hiroshima survivor:
   Countless people seeking water had crept to the river bank and died. Their chilled bodies became ice pillows for others, keeping them barely alive. Almost naked bodies floated by the hundreds in the river. . . . Volunteer wardens would touch a hand only to have the skin come away: there was no firm place to grasp. Of necessity, abandoning human dignity, they finally used gaff hooks to lift them onto trucks. . . .

3. Futaba Kitayama:
   By my side, many junior high school students, both boys and girls who were members of the volunteer corps, were squirming in agony. They were crying, insanely, "Mother! Mother!" They were so severely burned and blood-stained that one could scarcely dare to look at them.

4. A second-grade girl:
   My older brother went off to do compulsory labor and was never seen again. My younger brother was burned all over his body and died the following day. . . . Mother said she was going into town . . . we got there only to find that Mother had breathed her last a little earlier . . . that evening my older sister died. The day after her funeral my lovable younger sister passed away. . . . Father left this world on 10 September. . . .

5. Mitsuo Tomosawa:
   I have seen people who didn't have their bodies. They were wearing a helmet at that time and the skull was beneath the helmet. No bodies, just their skulls.

Thirty-three thousand bodies were sufficiently intact for burial or cremation. Thousands more floated out to sea. In three months the number of Hiroshima dead reached 130,000.

Nagasaki

Supported by a parachute, the bomb fell slowly. It required forty seconds to reach 1,700 feet above ground, at which point it exploded. Aimed by radar rather than sight because of the cloud bank, the bomb missed the center of Nagasaki* by 1 1/2 miles. Casualties were lighter than expected. In the first few minutes, 30,000 were killed. In the next four months, 40,000 more died from injuries.

In nearby Urakami prison, 134 prisoners and wardens died instantly. In the Urakami church, 200 members at confession and 20 priests died. Of the 1,500 children and teachers at Shiroyama primary school, 1,310 were killed. Thirteen hundred died at the nearby Yamazoto primary school. At Josei girls' school, 212 pupils and nuns died. Of the 1,800 doctors, nurses, students, and patients at Nagasaki College Hospital and the Medical College, over 1,000 died. Of 1,720 at the Mitsubishi steel works, 1,019 died; 2,250 died at the Mitsubishi ordnance factory. These deaths were mercifully quick—a matter of minutes.

Of all who were killed in Nagasaki, the large majority were the elderly, women and girls, and small children. Three percent of the dead were members of the Armed Forces.

1. A Nagasaki woman, her husband and their six children:
   On the third day, a friend of my husband came to help me salvage the debris of my home. We discovered a white, round object. An elderly passing soldier told us that it was the skull of a man in his thirties or forties. This must be my husband's, I realized. Dazed, we dug up six more skulls, and my children's butterfly badges with them.

2. Dr. Tatsuichiro Akizuki:
   I examined her . . . uncountable numbers of pieces of glass, one centimeter or two in length, had pierced the skin all over her back and penetrated the muscles. I seized a piece of glass with a pincette. I tried to pull it out, but failed . . . I managed to extract a sliver of glass, but the rest was deeply embedded.

Remember that these were small bombs—13 and 22 kilotons. Each bomb destroyed an area of 3 square miles. One Minuteman II missile

---

*Kokura, not Nagasaki, was the primary target. A dense cloud bank saved Kokura.

Nagasaki is a chilling illustration of Einstein's $E = mc^2$, relating binding energy E to mass m. At Nagasaki, less than 1/25 of an ounce of plutonium was converted to energy. But that minute mass was multiplied by c^2, the square of the speed of light.

will destroy 72 square miles, one Minuteman III missile with three Mark 12-A warheads will destroy 88 square miles, and one MX missile with ten Mark 12-A warheads (soon to come) will destroy 234 square miles.

Hard as it may be to believe, psychological damage to the Hibakusha (as the survivors are known in Japan) may have equalled physical damage. Children abandoned their dying parents, returning soldiers their terribly burned wives. Families were broken up, neighborhoods ceased to exist, community life ended, friends were dead or evacuated. All possessions were lost. Pathetic handwritten notices appeared throughout the ruins—"Has anyone seen Yoshiko?" Injuries or fear by employers of contamination ended chances for skilled employment anywhere; only unskilled work at very low pay was available. For ten years survivors got no help from the Japanese government (and, of course, none from the United States).

As time went on, fewer would marry them, and if they had children, even fewer would marry their children. The children continue to suffer from real and imagined inherited diseases; a common question is, "Why did you give birth to me?"

In Hiroshima alone, 1,000 to 2,000 orphaned children died from illness, injury, or hunger soon after the bomb. Five thousand others, many of whom did not know their own names, were found. Those who survived were soon discriminated against, and became alienated. The following was written by a young girl who had lost both parents:

Gradually I became quite gloomy, a cold-hearted person who rarely laughed. The sunsets in the country were beautiful. Everything was so fresh. Looking at so much beauty made me cry. I was starved for affection. Death. I could think of nothing but death.

Given the emphasis on family in Japanese society, the fate of the orphaned elderly (over 70, no possessions, completely alone) became equally tragic. We omit the scores of tales of untreated sickness, unrelieved pain, the plight of the bedridden, life in shacks, loneliness, and suicide.

TWO
Nuclear War

I can go into my office and pick up the telephone, and in twenty-five minutes seventy million people will be dead.
President Richard Nixon,
during Congressional impeachment proceedings

We live in the shadow of extinction.
Javier Perez de Cuellar,
Secretary-General of the United Nations

The Toll

Part One presents a simplistic scenario—the effect of a single bomb. But nuclear war may not be described by one bomb dropped on us by the Russians, and one dropped by us on them, with cooler heads stepping in and calling a halt. More likely it will be all-out, even if for no better reason than to destroy response.

What does all-out imply? Once again consider a single one-megaton nuclear bomb. Fatal third-degree and often fatal second-degree burns will afflict all persons within ten miles of burst, an area of 314 square miles. All structures within four or five miles will be leveled or heavily damaged, with death or serious injury to all within them. Lethal radiation over a much larger area will follow. The options are simple: death by blast, or death by heat, or death by fire, or death by radiation.

What is nuclear war? Multiply, if you can, the above by 5,000 for each country. That is nuclear war.

20

In 1965, Secretary of Defense Robert McNamara estimated 125 to 150 *million* American dead, and over 100 *million* Russian dead. Considering current nuclear megatonnage, these estimates are conservative. The 1977 estimate by the United States National Security Council was 140 million American dead and 113 million Russian dead, all within a few days. Dispersed population accounts for the lower Russian figures. Estimates by the United States Arms Control and Disarmament Agency are 105 to 130 million American dead and 80 to 95 million Russian dead. Estimates by the Congressional Office of Technology Assessment, for the first thirty days of a nuclear war, are up to 165 million American and 100 million Russian dead. *

Military analysts believe that the likely Soviet nuclear strike, before or after a nuclear strike by the United States, would be 5,000 megatons. Most warheads would be detonated near ground level at missile sites, air bases, and other military facilities. Along with destruction of nearby cities and the death of most of their inhabitants, five million square miles would be radioactive for months, possibly for years. Five million square miles is greater than the area of the United States. Even ground-burst nuclear attacks confined to silos housing American intercontinental ballistic missiles would hopelessly contaminate one million square miles. If all 2,000 likely targeted areas in the United States were attacked, with two small nuclear warheads exploded on each area, then, although no cities were directly assaulted, total American dead—those immediately dead following the attacks and those subsequently dead from the longer-term effects of radiation—would exceed 40 million; more dead than in all 130 wars fought on this planet since World War II. If two one-megaton warheads are exploded near each of the 1,050 ICBMs presently in silos (in South and North Dakota, Missouri, Kansas, Arkansas, Montana, Wyoming, and Arizona), all persons within two miles of each silo will die. Within four miles, all survivors of the blast will receive third-degree burns certain to be fatal; within nine miles, the second-degree burns likely under nuclear war conditions will also be fatal.

In December 1981, Dr. Herbert Abrams and William von Kaenel considered the medical consequences of a 6,559-megaton attack on the

---

*Total American dead in the Civil War, World War I, World War II, Korea, and Vietnam was 1 million. Total Russian dead in World War I, the 1918–1920 civil war, and World War II was 32 million.

United States; this megatonnage equals 505,000 Hiroshima bombs. The warhead distribution model was provided by the Federal Emergency Management Agency. During the first hour death will come via flash burns, trauma and blast injury, flame burns and smoke inhalation, and acute and fallout radiation. From the first day through four weeks, the sources of death will be flame burns and smoke inhalation, fallout radiation, lack of medical care, dehydration, communicable disease, exposure and hardship, and malnutrition. Later cancer* will be the major agent, and finally, for any (unlikely) future generations, genetic damage.

Moments after the attack, 86 million will be dead and 34 million will be severely injured. In the days and weeks following the attack, 50 million more will die.

Now consider the survivors. Twenty-three million will have received 200 or more rems of radiation; about the same number, 23 million, 100 to 200 rems. Most will soon die. As a consequence of severe radiation damage, those still alive will have reduced resistance to disease. High-incidence infectious diseases which, in epidemic form, may attack weakened survivors include diphtheria, hepatitis, influenza, meningitis, pneumonia, tuberculosis, and whooping cough. Lower-incidence diseases which may appear (or reappear!) in epidemic form include cholera, malaria, plague, shigellosis, smallpox, typhoid fever, typhus, and yellow fever. Among these, plague transmitted by rodents and their fleas— including bubonic plague transmitted by rats—has the prospect for a resurgence on an earth almost ideally enhanced by nuclear radiation. And not one state or federal laboratory able to identify this horror will likely be standing; all are in high-risk areas.

Now consider a nuclear strike on the Soviet Union. With plenty to spare, 1,350 Poseidon warheads, fewer than half of those deployed in our thirty-one Poseidon submarines, could, in thirty minutes, level all 220 Russian cities with a population over 100,000. In fact, *one* Poseidon submarine could destroy 160 of Russia's largest cities, dropping on each city three to seven times the megatonnage that fell on Hiroshima. *One* of our planned fleet of twenty to twenty-five Trident submarines, deploying 24 Trident 2 D5 missiles each with 9 warheads, could destroy

---

*A rise in the cancer rate as a consequence of nuclear war does not trouble Congressman Donald J. Mitchell of New York. It could be "countered by not rebuilding many of the cigarette plants that would be destroyed in such a holocaust."

216 Russian cities, with each receiving at least ten times the megatonnage that fell on Hiroshima. With the cities would go highways, railroads, electrical distribution, gas mains, petroleum, refineries, seaports, airports, and factories. And people.

According to one Pentagon estimate, reported by the Center for Defense Information, 100 nuclear warheads, delivered to Soviet Russia, could immediately kill 37 million and destroy 59% of Soviet industrial capacity. A second Pentagon estimate: a 2,000-megaton attack will kill half of the Soviet population and destroy two-thirds of Soviet industrial potential. Most of the industrial damage is accomplished by the first 100–200 megatons.

Nuclear War in Europe

Here is a reliable estimate of some of the consequences of nuclear war in Europe, a theater of high interest to American military strategists. We consider the explosion of 1,000 one-megaton nuclear weapons.

Total destruction, fire and blast:	50,000 square miles
Major destruction, fire and blast:	40,000 additional square miles
Damage, fire and blast:	Up to 250,000 additional square miles
Fatalities, direct effect of explosion:	Over 200,000,000 persons*
Fallout, lethal to unprotected persons:	300,000 square miles
Fallout, significant contamination:	Several million additional square miles

The Years That Follow

If 50% of the nuclear arsenals of the United States and the Soviet Union are detonated in the northern hemisphere, the ozone layer in the northern hemisphere will be depleted by 70% to 80%, in the southern hemisphere by 40%. Unless they remain permanently indoors, all men, women, and children will be permanently blinded. Another and even more frightening estimate by Dr. Tsipis: If 10% to 20% of the

---

*Roger Molander, who founded Ground Zero, attended a meeting at the Pentagon at which a Navy captain remarked that people were "talking as if nuclear war would be the end of the world when, in fact, only 500 million people would be killed."

world's current nuclear arsenal is detonated, *all* unprotected men, women, children, and animals will be blinded by glare.

Radioactive fallout would severely affect open areas far beyond the attack zone. Few farm animals could be sheltered; those left outside would slowly die from radioactive dust and debris. In springtime, plant growth would be halted by radiation; crops would wilt or be poisonous. For surviving farm workers, fallout would lead to radiation sickness, weakness, and early death. Food markets and transportation would have largely disappeared. The surviving family, even the distant farm family, would have to revert to something close to Stone Age existence.

Nuclear Winter

In 1983, Carl Sagan and his associates reached even gloomier conclusions. They consider the explosion of five thousand to ten thousand megatons likely figures in a major nuclear war.* The blast alone will immediately kill 750,000,000 humans; 1,100,000,000 will die from blast or fire or immediate radiation, most of them even before the mushroom cloud dissipates. Another 1,100,000,000 will be sufficiently injured to require medical attention (which they are unlikely to get). Thousands more will soon die from the poisoned atmosphere; everything flammable will ignite, and the burning of stored synthetic chemicals will release carbon monoxide, dioxin, and cyanides.

For most of the two to three billion humans who survive all this, a grim, but likely brief, life lies ahead. Darkness will set in. For each megaton of explosion, 100,000 to 600,000 tons of dust particles will fill the air. Add 250,000,000 tons of smoke particles. Both dust and smoke will remain in the stratosphere for a year or more, blotting out the sun, sending temperatures in the northern hemisphere down to $-45°F$, no matter what the season.† Plants and seeds will die; streams, ponds, and reservoirs will be topped by three feet of ice. Millions will die of starvation and thirst. All support systems will vanish—food,

---

*Even a "minor" nuclear war is noteworthy. If 100 megatons (less than 1% of the explosive power of the global strategic nuclear arsenal) are exploded over one thousand cities, the effect will almost equal that associated with 5,000 megatons.

†$-45°F$ for four months, $-9°F$ for nine months, $+27°F$ for one year. The explosion of no more than 500 to 2,000 of the world inventory of 20,000 strategic nuclear weapons could produce such temperatures.

shelter, energy, transport, medical care, communication. Lethal radiation will finish off most of the final few survivors. Sagan's group concludes that there may be *no* survivors in the northern hemisphere. And, given the megatonnage of nuclear arsenals soon to come, these estimates may be conservative. The group writes:

Extinction of the human species itself cannot be excluded.

Four Soviet scientists[*] came to Washington in December 1983 and stated that their own studies agree with those of Sagan and his associates.

One of the minor long-term casualties of a nuclear war will be a decline of interest in economic and political forms, and an end to the myth that the bomb could settle the issue between capitalism and communism. As Kenneth Galbraith has made clear, both of these political forms require technology and organization. There will be neither. Alongside an erosion of the will, let alone the ability to live, alongside acres of corpses which can only suggest that life itself has lost meaning, the salient political issue of our time will be lost in the rubble. Carl Sagan writes, "The ashes of communism and capitalism will be indistinguishable."

Shelters

In a nuclear war, occupants of family shelters will die in assorted ways: by crushing if the shelter is vulnerable to bomb blast; by incineration if the shelter is reached by the firestorm (at five miles from burst, shelter temperature could reach 1,500 degrees Fahrenheit); by asphyxiation if the firestorm absorbs all available oxygen; by starvation or dehydration in the likely absence of radiation-free food or water; or by initial radiation if the air within the shelter cannot be continuously filtered.

MIT physicists estimate that appearance outside a shelter for more

---

[*]Yevgeny Velikhov, vice president of the Soviet Academy of Sciences; Alexander Pavlov, director of the Moscow Scientific Institute on Roentgenology and Radiology; Vladimir Aleksandrov, head of the Climate Research Laboratory of Climate Modeling at the Computing Center of the Soviet Academy of Sciences; and Sergei Kapitza, professor of physics at the Moscow Physico-Technical Institute.

than three minutes will produce fatal third-degree burns from intense ultraviolet light; this is the consequence of ozone layer depletion.

For those at a greater distance from burst, protection in a family shelter could provide a small improvement in chances for survival. But it will be small indeed. Living mostly in darkness, unable to communicate with others attempting to survive, with radiation gradually penetrating the shelter, occupants might gain several extra weeks or even months of what could arguably be called life. Lacking means, they will not be able to determine the level of radioactive contamination of stored food; one choice will be between hunger and radiation sickness. Toilet refuse and vomit from those gradually being afflicted with some degree of radiation sickness will add extra stench to the stale air of the shelter. Any early exposure to radiation will have weakened or destroyed the immune system; even minor infections will take hold and bring death.* Any injuries or burns of those who were late reaching the shelter will be far beyond the range of any first-aid kit. With five or more people in the space of a bathroom,† emotion eruption, alternating with demoralization and apathy, is virtually guaranteed. At best, many occupants of family shelters will find themselves alive in what will turn out,

---

*Here is a medically appropriate program, developed by Dr. Gould Andrews, for handling *isolated* cases of such infections. The reader will have to imagine how much of this program can be applied to hundreds of thousands, struggling to survive either in shelters or in the radioactive rubble that once included hospitals.

Immediately after diagnosis of exposure to 100 rad ($\approx$rem) or more:
Avoid hospitalizing patient except in sterile environment facility. Look for preexisting infections and obtain cultures of suspicious areas—consider especially carious teeth, gingivae, skin, and vagina. Culture a clean-caught urine specimen. Culture stool specimen for identification of all organisms; run appropriate sensitivity tests for *Staph. aureus* and Gram-negative rods. Treat any infection that is discovered. Start oral nystatin to reduce *Candida* organisms. Do HLA typing of patient's family, especially siblings, to select HLA-matched leukocyte and platelet donors for later need.

If granulocyte count falls to less than 1,500/mm³:
Start oral antibiotics—vancomycin 500 mg liquid P.O. q. 4 hr, gentamycin 200 mg liquid P.O. q. 4 hr, nystatin 1×10^6 units liquid P.O. 4 hr, 4×10^6 units as tablets P.O. q. 4 hr. Isolate patient in laminar flow room or life island. Daily antiseptic bath and shampoo with chlorhexidine gluconate. Trim fingers and toenails carefully and scrub area daily. For female patients, daily Betadine douche and insert one nystatin vaginal tablet b.i.d. Culture nares, oropharynx, urine, stool, and skin of groins and axillae twice weekly. Culture blood if fever over 101 degrees F.

†Including the dead. The Federal Emergency Management Agency (FEMA) is currently studying the merits of body bags vs. graves dug in advance.

in short time, to be their coffins. The delay will be shorter for children.*

At the federal level, the 1982 budget provided $148 million for shelters to protect a handful of the bureaucracy, $252 million for all others. In the request by FEMA for $4.2 billion for its "seven-year program," shelter construction costs were not even included; the request was turned down by Congress. Another proposal: blast shelters for the four million "essential" workers, at a cost of $10 billion, no shelters for the 232 million inessential.

Evacuation

I just can't understand why people can't grasp such a simple concept. Get our American people away from where the bombs are going to go off.

Congressman Donald J. Mitchell of New York,
whose antidote to rising cancer rates is quoted earlier in this book.

Any page spent on evacuation is a page wasted. The Federal Emergency Management Agency has scores of plans for evacuation. Were they not macabre, they would be humorous. A few examples will suffice.

In the event of a nuclear attack, the current FEMA plan requires most of the 103,000 residents of Alexandria, Virginia to make their way to a town of 1,000 in West Virginia named Webster Springs. On learning this, and at the invitation of the Director of the Woodchopping Festival, the vice-mayor of Alexandria decided to visit Webster Springs— seven hours away on a road with hairpin turns, washed-out bridges, virtually no gas stations, sometimes one lane wide. No one in Webster Springs had heard of the plan, but, in the spirit of cooperation, the residents promised to set aside their forty motel rooms. Anyone who could not be accommodated would be assigned a tree.

FEMA's plan for Tucson, Arizona calls for some part of the popu-

---

*Detailed British analysis of shelter life leaves little to imagination. Handling of the shelter dead, defense against forced entry by those without shelters, explosion of rat and insect populations, the impact of radiation-resistant viruses and bacteria, early shelter symptoms (nausea, vomiting, fever, diarrhea), later shelter symptoms (bleeding gums, hair falling out . . .). Finally, an estimate of prolonged life—several weeks.

lation to make it to Nogales; once there, 542 Tucson residents are to be lodged in Ed Baez's True Value hardware store. No one from FEMA had informed Baez but on being interviewed he had no objection. He thought there might be plumbing problems. He also thought that he might go over the hill to Mexico.

FEMA's New York City plan calls for 614,600 residents of the Bronx, few of whom own automobiles, to drive north on Interstate 87, a highway unlikely to exist. Some 43,200 residents of Queens are to proceed to LaGuardia Airport, where they will board several hundred (likely nonexistent) planes for Bradford, Pennsylvania. From Manhattan, 300,000 are to proceed by subway (!) to Hoboken, New Jersey; from there they will travel by railroad boxcars to safety.*

After "an effective national relocation plan" along these lines, FEMA states that immediate deaths can be held down to 45,000,000.

In a nuclear war, the federal government has estimated that 100 million people will need to be evacuated, most of them from major urban areas. With at most thirty minutes' warning, there will be nowhere to go, no way to get there. And in the event of any plan for *early* mass evacuation, remember that the enemy can retarget in minutes. Remember, too, that it is likely that every American city with a population as low as 25,000 has already been targeted.

Here are some helpful suggestions, taken from the endless supply of evacuation and shelter plans issued by FEMA; they should provide comic relief at the moment of serious injury or death.

Take the time you need to pack.
Prepare your home as if you were leaving for a vacation.
Draw your curtains and drapes.
Take along all perishables.
Take a portable toilet with you.
Fifteen double bed sheets should be in each shelter.
Bring your credit cards.

If you are at work,

---

*One hundred and ten areas in the United States, including the entire state of Maryland, have opted out of FEMA's tragicomic evacuation plans. For a lucid account of the federal government's plans for surviving a nuclear war see *The Day After World War III*, by Edward Zuckerman.

All shift workers should stay on their jobs until the end of their shifts.

And if anyone becomes ill,

Get a physician to treat the patient as soon as possible,

to which the Civil Defense Director of the United States adds,

Care for radiation casualties includes bedrest, nursing . . .

As the bomb falls, the Post Office requires all of us to leave forwarding addresses. As specified in the Postal Service manual, that includes escaped mental patients and convicts. Knowing where we are will also help the Internal Revenue Service, which announced that it will resume collection of federal taxes thirty days after the onset of nuclear war.

THREE
How Many
Nuclear Weapons?

American and Russian Stockpiles

You have seen what one or more nuclear weapons can do. How many nuclear weapons are *ready for use?*

The United States has over 11,000 strategic (long-range, intercontinental) nuclear warheads. The Soviet Union has over 8,000. The following breakdown shows the Soviets favoring land-based, the Americans submarine-based.

	Strategic Nuclear Weapons	
	USA	*USSR*
land-based	2,100	5,800
submarine-based	5,540	2,100
bombers	3,550	340
	11,190	8,240

American strategic weapons total over 4,000 megatons in explosive yield, Soviet strategic weapons total close to 8,000 megatons. The higher megatonnage describes the Soviet attempt to compensate for American superiority in accuracy. *

---

*The largest nuclear bomb ever constructed—58 megatons—was exploded by the Russians in 1962. A larger bomb was not considered; its underground explosion might have broken all the windows in Moscow—4,000 miles away.

The United States can explode about 13,600 nuclear weapons on Soviet Russia; 11,190 strategic weapons noted above plus approximately 2,400 nuclear weapons either on aircraft carriers or deliverable by tactical aircraft from (nearby) Europe. The Soviet Union can explode about 8,500 nuclear weapons on the United States; 8,240 strategic nuclear weapons noted above plus 260 nuclear weapons deliverable by Backfire bombers—from (distant) Russia, on one-way flights.

The United States has 11,100 intermediate-range and tactical (short-range, theater, battlefield) nuclear weapons, the Soviet Union (probably) 10,000 intermediate and tactical weapons.

Total Nuclear Weapons

	USA	USSR
strategic	11,190	8,240
intermediate and tactical	11,100	10,000
	22,290	18,240

Of American intermediate and tactical nuclear weapons, 1,300 are deployed at sea, 350 are in the Pacific, 5,800 are in Europe, and 3,600 are stockpiled at home.

The current American total nuclear stockpile adds up to about 8,000,000,000 tons of TNT, equal to 615,000 Hiroshima bombs. The world nuclear stockpile may be close to 1,500,000 Hiroshima bombs.

The two following tables show the core ingredients of American and Soviet *strategic* nuclear weapons strength. These tables do not include thousands of intermediate-range, short-range, and antisubmarine nuclear weapons. The major sources were the Center for Defense Information, Institute for Defense and Disarmament Studies, and the Pentagon.

The Next Ten Years: New Nuclear Weapons

With its current nuclear arsenal, the United States can blow up the entire world in less than forty-five minutes. And repeatedly; the most careful estimate is twelve times. So can the Soviet Union, perhaps six times. The United States can destroy, fifty times over, all Russian cities with populations over 100,000. If a Soviet first strike wiped out 93% of American intercontinental ballistic missiles and *all* American bomb-

Strategic Nuclear Weapons
United States

number of missiles	weapons per missile	kilotons per weapon	weapons deployed
land-based missiles			
550 Minuteman III improved	3	335	1,650
450 Minuteman II	1	1,000–1,500	450
33 Titan II	1	9,000	32
submarine-based missiles			
304 Poseidon	10	40	3,040
312 Trident I	8	100	2,496
bombers			
264 B52G/H	4	100–1,000	3,200
61 FB111	2	100–1,000	360

ers not on alert and *all* American strategic submarines not on patrol, the United States could, without difficulty and within thirty minutes, completely destroy Soviet Russia's twenty-two largest cities and kill almost everyone in them. *

This would seem to be adequate nuclear firepower. But the United States plans to build more powerful and/or more effective nuclear weapons. By 1992 approximately 17,000 new nuclear weapons will appear in the American arsenal, adding to or replacing nuclear weapons in current inventory. The likely breakdown, by the Center for Defense Information, is shown in the table on page 35; numbers are rounded.

The heavily researched *Nuclear Weapons Databook, Volume 1: U.S. Nuclear Forces and Capabilities*, by Thomas Cochran, William Arkin, and Milton Hoenig estimates new replacement nuclear warheads for the coming decade to be close to 29,000; these include up to fifteen new warhead types. (See table on page 34.)

---

*In fact, 200 nuclear weapons are sufficient to make most of the world uninhabitable for at least one year. *Bulletin of the Atomic Scientists* estimates that 200 to 300 nuclear weapons are sufficient "to impoverish a continent for hundreds of years."

Strategic Nuclear Weapons
Soviet Russia

number of missiles	weapons per missile	kilotons per weapon	weapons deployed
land-based missiles			
520 SS11	1	1,000	520
60 SS13	1	1,000	60
20 SS17	1		20
130 SS17	4	550	600
23 SS18	1	10,000	23
100 SS18	8	550	800
185 SS18	10	550	1,850
30 SS19	1	1,000	30
330 SS19	6	550	1,980
submarine-based missiles			
368 SSN 6	1	1,000	368
292 SSN 8	1	1,000	292
12 SSN X17	1	1,000	12
75 SSN 18	3	200	225
125 SSN 18	7	200	875
24 SSN 18	1	—	24
40 SSN 20	7.5 (average)	—	300
bombers			
100 TU95	2	750	200
30 TU95	2	1,000	60
43 Mya-4	1	1,000	43

New Nuclear Weapons
United States 1983–1993

1983	in production	11,700
1983–88	planned	4,200
late 1980s–90s		12,700
		28,600

MX

An expensive example of senseless nuclear defense (or nuclear offense) for the 1980s is the MX missile, proposed successor to Minuteman III. Minuteman III has three warheads per missile, 170–335 kilotons per warhead, a range of 8,000 miles, and is accurate to 700 feet. MX has ten to fourteen warheads* per missile, 300 kilotons per warhead, about the same range as Minuteman III but with accuracy to 200–300 feet. One hundred MX were to be built and deployed by 1989, forty to all of them temporarily stored in hardened Minuteman III silos. † But in the spring of 1984, the House of Representatives reduced the number from 40 to 15, the latter to be funded only if the Soviet Union fails to return to the bargaining table. The Senate supported 21 missiles with no conditions. The issue may be resolved in 1985.

For fiscal 1984, the MX budget reached $5 billion, including research and development. The construction budget over five years will be $15–20 billion.

With hardened silos (dense pack), plane launch, deep tunnel, shallow trench, randomly moving railway cars, underwater launch, or any other base plan, the MX program could reach $75 billion. And given the history of Air Force cost estimates, that is on the low side. At a stage in MX development at which the Air Force estimate of cost was $24 billion, the director of military research of the Council on Economic Priorities estimated the cost at $104–232 billion.

MX is accurate. But pinpoint accuracy in nuclear weaponry is hardly necessary when bombing military installations or industrial areas. It is useful only when planning to strike narrowly defined objectives, notably

---

*This makes MX an even more attractive target—with one hit the enemy can expect to eliminate ten to fourteen warheads.

†A standard argument for MX: Should air-based and sea-based nuclear weaponry (on which we have spent billions of dollars) fail, we can fall back on the best land-based nuclear weapon (MX). Exactly the same argument has been made for air-based and for sea-based nuclear weaponry.

New Nuclear Weapons
United States 1983–1992

for land-based missiles	
Pershing II	380
MX	1,060
antiballistic	500
for submarines and ships	
Trident 1	1,440
Trident 2	1,440
antiaircraft	500
antisubmarine	1,650
for Cruise missiles	
ground launched	560
sea launched	760
air launched and advanced missiles	3,500
for aircraft	
strategic bombers	2,500
various	1,000
for battlefield use	
8″ artillery	800
155mm artillery	1,000
	17,090

missile-filled Russian silos. Knowing this, to save its own missiles from destruction, the Soviets will have to consider a first strike of their own. Even this appalling first-strike scenario is fatal to all concerned; the recipient of the first strike, whomever, will have sufficient time (ten to thirty minutes) to reply with his own silo-based missiles. No missiles will be caught in silos.* No first-strike or second-strike country will win anything. Either way, annihilation is guaranteed for both.

Former CIA chief Admiral Stansfield Turner writes:

---

*The intense debate on bases for MX missiles (in part due to the slow launch of MX, in part simply an Air Force-Navy struggle for power) is largely irrelevant. Viewed either as a first-strike or a second-strike weapon, MX bases will matter little; the missiles will have been fired.

It seems ironical to try to reduce the probability of someone starting a nuclear war, when you are building a weapon like the MX that drives the superpowers to a hairtrigger response.

Cruise and Pershing II

We have already produced Cruise and Pershing II nuclear missiles, whose current deployment in Western Europe has turned the streets of European cities into battlegrounds.

The Cruise missile can be constructed to be ground, sea, underwater, or air launched. It is low-flying, therefore satellite and radar evasive. It will be difficult to verify the number of Cruise missiles in flight or their positions.

The ground-launched Cruise missile (GLCM) mounts one 10 to 50 kiloton nuclear warhead, has a speed of 500–600 miles per hour, a range of up to 1,000–1,500 miles, and accuracy to within 100–300 feet. At maximum kilotonnage, each missile has the destructive power of four Hiroshima bombs.

The deployment of 464 ground-launched Cruise missiles in Western Europe began in December 1983. Distribution of the missiles:

West Germany	96
Great Britain	160
Sicily	112
Belgium	48
The Netherlands*	48
	464

The Navy wants 4,000 sea-launched Cruise missiles (SLCM), at least 700 to 1,000 of them armed with up to 200 kiloton nuclear warheads; estimated cost $13–$15 billion, over $3 million each. Through 1990, the Air Force wants 1,800 air-launched Cruise missiles (ALCM); estimated cost $5 billion, close to $3 million each. Some cost estimates reach $5 million–$10 million per missile. The Air Force reduced its earlier Cruise order (Boeing) from 4,300 to 1,800, purchasing instead the advanced Stealth bomber (General Dynamics).

---

*In June 1984, by a vote of 79 to 71, the Dutch Parliament delayed deployment to 1988.

Beginning in December 1983, 108 Pershing II missiles were deployed in West Germany; in fact, by January 1984, nine Pershing II missiles were already operational. Each missile has one 10–20 kiloton warhead, current range 1,000–2,000 miles, high accuracy 65–130 feet. It can drill nine stories into the ground while exploding. Cost, about $5 million each. Speed is 6,000 miles per hour; from West Germany to the Soviet border in five minutes, to the hardened silos just west of Moscow in nine minutes. This will, of course, lead to a hair-trigger missile launch alert on the part of the Russians.

Consider computer error and the Pershing II. Essentially, nuclear bombs are computer-controlled. An error in Soviet computers—which are notably less reliable than our own—incorrectly indicating that Pershing II's have been fired, and the Soviets will have nine minutes to decide whether to die alone or to fire off their own missiles and take the United States and a good part of the Western world with them. The reader may decide which course of action is the more likely. Note the curious but important fact that unreliability in *Soviet* computers increases *American* vulnerability.

Cruise and Pershing II missiles are profitable items. They are assembled from parts manufactured by several hundred American subcontractors, most of whom you never heard of—even the larger suppliers. One example: Williams Research Corporation in Walled Lake, Michigan, with contracts close to $700 million. As usual, final assembly takes place at the Department of Energy's Pantex plant outside Amarillo, Texas.

These are two more of the current deadly additions to the nuclear warhead inventory of the United States.

The Next Ten Years: Cost

The amount of money now spent on arms is beyond comprehension. In 1984 the United States will spend $200 billion. Over the next three years, the United States will spend almost $1 billion *daily* on the military. The $1.9 trillion the United States plans to spend on arms over the next five years would more than pay off our entire national debt; moreover, recent estimates by the General Accounting Office raise the five-year figure to $2 trillion ($2,000,000,000,000). If you spent $1 million every day for the next 1,985 *years*, you would not spend one-half of what President Reagan plans to allocate to the military over the next five years.

At the world level the facts are no less incredible. The $550 billion spent by the world on arms in 1981 equaled that year's income of the poorest half (2.3 billion people) of the world. The 1985 figure will equal $1 trillion. The arms race now costs the world over $2 billion *daily*. On research, development and production of nuclear arms alone, the world has already spent $900 billion.

The following table shows costs of forthcoming American nuclear weapons, roughly over the 1980s and early 1990s. Weaponry is classified differently than in the previous table, and certain entries in the previous table are made more explicit.

The lower figures add up to $318 billion, the higher figures $458 billion.

Cost of American Nuclear Weapons over the 1980s and Early 1990s

weapon system	first year deployed	total cost (billions $)
MX	1987	27–75
Trident Submarine	1982	40
Trident 1 missile	1979	11
Trident 2 missile	1989	37–50
B-1B bomber	1986	40
Stealth bomber	1990	40–50
B52 alterations	ongoing	6
ALCM	1982	5
GLCM	1983	4
SLCM	1984	12
Advanced Cruise	1988	7
Pershing II	1983	3
Command, Control, Communications	ongoing	40–50
Air defense	ongoing	8–35
Midgetman	1992	38–70

If these massive expenditures are part of an effort to bankrupt the Soviet Union, they may not be altogether without success. To some degree, the following declines are the consequence of heavy nuclear arms expenditures by Soviet Russia.

time period	annual growth of Soviet GNP
1950s	6%
1960s	5%
1971–1975	4%
1976–1979	3%

As Tom Wicker of *The New York Times* writes, the Reagan philosophy has been, "Outspend the Russians in an arms race, and they'll come to us on their knees." An illusion, and a dangerous one.

Profit and waste are hallmarks of American weaponry. Prime contracts are written cost plus; profit is simply a fixed percentage of cost.* And with cost overruns reaching 320%, substantial profit is assured.† On MX, prime contracts were awarded even before an MX program existed.

---

*As the Center for Defense Information writes, "There is absolutely no incentive to keep prices low; on the contrary, the higher the price charged by the subcontractor, the greater the mark-up by the prime contractor and the larger the profits all around." Here are examples of subcontractor charges:

	standard price	price paid	number of overcharges
circuit breaker	$11	$243	22
push switch	$15	$241	15
semiconductor	4¢	$110	2,750
resistor	5¢	$100	2,000
transistor	24¢	$75	312
tube	$12	$639	53
case assembly	$6,446	$45,236	7
oil plug	$117	$1,050	9
connector	$13	$143	11
soldering iron	$4	$272	73
tape measure	$10	$427	42
hammer	$18	$450	24

†Substantial indeed. Over 1981–1983, five of the top dozen American military contractors reported profits totaling $10.5 billion. None paid federal taxes. The contractors were Grumman, Lockheed, General Dynamics, General Electric, and Boeing. The top dozen paid taxes of $296 million on reported profits of $19 billion—about 1.5%.

Research and development costs are covered by the Pentagon. Outside experts, particularly critical experts, are excluded by secrecy clauses. Congressional understanding and analysis of the costs of nuclear weaponry are minimal. The life of nuclear weaponry is attractively brief; some nuclear programs become obsolete while the weapons are still in the development stage. The story is endless; only details change. (a) The Air Force bought 200 arm rests at $670 each. An Air Force private determined that they could be constructed at the base for $5 to $25 each. His proposal was rejected as "not in the best interests of the Air Force." (b) Between the first and third orders for spare parts for an Army anti-aircraft gun, prices rose almost 2000%. (c) At Rockwell, certain labor costs on the B1 bomber were in fact $15 per hour; the Pentagon was billed at almost $200 per hour. At Boeing, certain labor costs on the Cruise missile were in fact $14 per hour; the Pentagon was billed at $114 per hour. (d) In four months an equipment specialist picked $1.5 million of new parts out of trashbins. (e) $74,000 for an aluminum ladder. (f) In 1981 a $1 plastic cap for a stool leg cost $1,086. In 1984, the price rose to $1,118. (g) A ten-cup coffee brewer at $7,000, explained by the supplier as follows:

material	$2,856
labor	1,121
overhead	1,760
administrative	718
profit	548
	$7,003

Ernest Fitzgerald, a well-known Air Force management deputy, estimates Department of Defense waste at $30 billion–$50 billion annually.*

Accounting and organizational deception is routine. According to the General Accounting Office, 25% of NASA's multibillion-dollar budget is spent on Pentagon programs. Nuclear warheads are not billed to the Pentagon. They are charged against the Department of Energy's "nuclear defense" budget. In fiscal 1982 that budget was $5 billion, with 80% going to weapons and weapons materials.

---

*Some part of this huge waste can be credited to the size of the operation. The Department of Defense averages 56,000 new contracts every working *day*.

Military spending is inflationary. No matter what the state of the economy, military purchases are certain to be approved, generally to be financed by federal deficits. And no community-useful consumer or producer goods emerge. Moreover, and contrary to military claims, repeated studies reveal little technological spinoff; the specialized technology that goes into building a nuclear bomb has had slight impact on nonmilitary production technique.

Finally, consider the waste of natural and human resources, and the alternative uses that could have been made of the money spent. Payment for the life-threatening list of nuclear devices to be acquired during the 1980s will come out of funds once available for lifesaving. Programs for the poor, for children, for the elderly, for the sick and disabled, for minorities, for education, for crime prevention, for energy, and for the unemployed—all have been severely cut to pay for totally unnecessary additional nuclear weapons. A single example: The MX budget for one year—fiscal 1983—would more than cover *all* items below, *all* of which were cut from the fiscal 1983 Reagan budget.

Medicaid	$680	million
Child nutrition	280	"
Food for women and children	70	"
Legal services	70	"
Supplemental Security Income	430	"
Education	350	"
Student loans	660	"
Pell grants to low-income students	120	"
Energy and conservation	360	"
Community development	510	"
Mass transit	500	"
Economic development	70	"
Food stamps	920	"
Aid to families with children	950	"

Star Wars

Space is the new high ground of battle.

Lieutenant General Richard C. Henry, retired,
Deputy Commander of Space Command,
United States Air Force

If you think the preceding list will satisfy President Reagan and the Pentagon, you are wrong. Space will be the battlefield of the 1990s* and the price will be high. Of a total of $165 billion spent on space since 1958, over $50 billion went to space weaponry. In 1983 the Pentagon planned to spend $15 billion to $18 billion over the next five years on space-based weaponry. In 1984 that figure was raised to $26 billion. And that, as we shall see, is only the beginning.

Here are five competing current proposals for a *defensive* space warfare system.

1. Space-based chemical lasers, powered by hydrogen and fluorine, pointed and focused by large mirrors ground to near-perfect reflectivity. Dr. Kosta Tsipis estimates cost and time required to get the necessary laser fuel into orbit at $100 billion and 100 years. Continuous coverage of the USSR would require about fifty lasers; fuel for them would require 1,000 shuttle flights.

2. Ground-based lasers† guided by huge—anywhere from thirty feet in diameter to the roof of the Superdome—mirrors orbiting in space. A trifling amount of water vapor or dirt on the mirrors, readily delivered by the enemy, will produce major misdirection.

3. X-ray lasers, powered by small nuclear explosions, a system proposed by Dr. Edward Teller. The laser battle stations themselves could be launched into space by a new breed of submarines. X-ray lasers are capable of purging the sky of just about everything in it.‡ But with each launch the delivery system is destroyed. For their development over the next five years, $895 million has been set aside.

4. Beams of charged particles, for example, protons and electrons. It is not yet clear that such beams could hit an object one million times the size of an ICBM. Moreover, particle beams produce secondary radiation which could be as devastating as a nuclear attack. Roald Sagdeyev, Director of the Institute for Cosmic Research of the Soviet Academy of Sciences,

---

*The United States and the Soviet Union each has about 100 orbiting satellites, many providing *military* information. Approximately 50% of major current space ventures by the USA and the USSR are military.

†Laser beams have been adapted to ground-level conventional warfare. The United States Army has developed "an effective instrument of terror," a noiseless, odorless low-powered laser which produces vitreal hemorrhage, permanently blinding enemy soldiers up to one mile distant. Production was halted in 1984.

‡In 1984, about 3,800 man-made objects.

who views any space defense system as impossible, remarks, "Particle beams are even more stupid than lasers."

5. "High Frontier" defense, favored by Lieutenant General Daniel Graham, retired chief of the Defense Intelligence Agency and a leader of the American space weapons team.* 432 battle stations, orbiting 500 miles out. Considering gaps in coverage, the more likely number of battle stations would be 1,000. Each station carries 40 to 45 kill vehicles. A program of immense cost. And high vulnerability; small, inexpensive space mines could orbit alongside the battle stations and be exploded on command.

Any system of space weapons will be very costly. One laser system, capable of destroying one thousand incoming nuclear warheads, is on the drawing board; the cost could reach $500 billion. One variant is a constellation of space laser platforms which might intercept 50% of attacking intercontinental missiles; $200 billion to build, $50 billion annually to maintain.

The American space weapons team has the explicit support of President Reagan. To get started on a "multi-satellite global ballistic missile defense system"—to intercept and destroy enemy ICBMs—General Graham required $35 billion.†

The Pentagon speaks of a three-level laser space defense system. The cost would be incredible, likely close to $1,000,000,000,000,000. But assume that over the next ten years this system is constructed. Assume that each of the three levels of defense will be 80% effective, a figure far higher than any current estimate. Now consider a full-scale nuclear war in which we are attacked by 10,000 nuclear missiles. The outer layer of defense destroys 8,000 of them. Of the 2,000 that get through, 1,600 are destroyed by the middle layer of defense. Of the 400 that get through the middle layer, 320 are destroyed by the final layer, leaving 80 missiles (some of which may mount multiple warheads) to explode over America, many more than enough to destroy our country and every one of us.

Dr. Robert Bowman, who headed the Air Force advanced space

---

*In March 1984, Lieutenant-General James Abrahamson was appointed by the Secretary of Defense to lead the Strategic Defense Initiative Organization.

†An early step; the United States Air Force has already been directed to have in operation by 1987 an antisatellite squadron. It will include twelve F-15 fighters, equipped to launch 28 small explosive-loaded interceptor satellites.

program 1976–1978 and whose studies provide much of the material of this section, offers his view of President Reagan's plan to develop defensive space weaponry:

All have staggering technical problems. All are likely to cost on the order of a trillion dollars. . . . All violate one or more existing treaties. All are extremely vulnerable. All are subject to a variety of countermeasures. All could be made impotent by alternative offensive missiles, such as cruise missiles. All could be overwhelmed by large numbers of offensive missiles and therefore would be likely to reignite the numerical arms race in offensive weapons. All would (if they worked) be more effective as part of a first strike than against one. . . . Most importantly, all would be extremely destabilizing, probably triggering the nuclear war which both sides are trying to prevent.

All defensive space programs have the same attractive mission—to destroy enemy ICBMs before they reach their targets. But no *defensive* system makes fundamental sense. In space weaponry, advantage always rests with the offense. The offense can choose how, when and where. Note also that a single intermediate-level nuclear explosion in space will destroy *any* defensive system.

In the judgment of Richard DeLauer, Undersecretary of Defense for Research, *each* one of eight remaining unsolved space weaponry problems would require for solution an effort as great as or greater than that required to put a man on the moon. Dr. Tsipis, who is also associate director of MIT's Program in Science and Technology for International Security, remarks, "Proposals for the erection of a laser antiballistic missile defense in space sound like little more than childlike, wishful fantasies of omnipotence . . ." Nobel laureate Hans Bethe describes current claims for missile defense systems as "totally science fiction."

In April 1984, the Congressional Office of Technology Assessment concluded that the prospect for success of a space-based antimissile system is "so remote that it should not serve as the basis of public expectation or national policy." The Office was "extremely pessimistic" because of the likelihood of (a) Soviet countermeasures, (b) failure to protect against bombers carrying nuclear weapons and (c) low-flying Cruise-type missiles.

"Never before," writes Dr. Bowman, "has a President faced with such a monumental decision been so shielded from the truth." He continues:

No one seems to have explained to the President the great vulnerability of these systems, nor the many countermeasures available to render them useless, nor the numerous alternative means for delivering nuclear weapons. No one has told him how an arms race in space would multiply the danger of accidental war. No one has explained to him that possession of such "defensive" weapons by both sides (since they could destroy each other with the speed of light) would make war inevitable and immediate. In short, no one has told him that even if the technology problems were overcome, and these weapons made to work as advertised, they could not protect us from nuclear weapons, but would be likely to bring on the war which we do not want and could not survive.

There is more. Electronic reconnaissance satellites 60,000 miles out in space, as well as devices to destroy them. Earthbound innovations include railguns, sensors, death sprays. These sensors are intelligence-gathering devices in variety; acoustic, seismic, magnetic, chemical, radar, infrared. They include radio-frequency transmitters disguised as animal droppings, hand-placed along paths, trails, and roads. The death sprays are minute droplets which produce death via heart attack.*

One *offensive* space war system (NAVSTAR) consists of eighteen interlocked satellites which would guide submarine-launched ballistic missiles. Via continuous monitoring of the position and velocity of the missiles, much higher accuracy than currently possible can be reached. Such improved accuracy, coupled with relative immunity from Soviet surveillance, would be useful in one action only—a first strike on Soviet missiles still in their silo bases. The construction of such a space guidance system by the United States would produce an immediate and obvious Soviet reaction; Soviet silo-based nuclear weapons would go on hair-trigger alert—use them or lose them. In short, another major step on the road to accidental or planned nuclear war.

Binary Nerve Gas and Germ Warfare

Two weapons, prospects for our ultimate arsenal, are worthy of notice; they are binary nerve gas and germ warfare. They are non-nuclear, but both have the potential to become worldwide destroyers of people and animals.

---

*This is merely one of the biological or chemical weapons currently available or under consideration. For a detailed (and shocking) account, see Brian Beckett, *Weapons of Tomorrow*.

Binary nerve gas leaves unharmed protected combatants; it kills un-protected civilians. A single microscopic drop is lethal. But death does not come easily. The only printable symptoms are uncontrollable vom-iting, urination, and defecation, convulsions and paralysis. If one is fortunate, coma is followed by death from asphyxiation within fifteen minutes.

President Reagan has stated that nerve gas weapons are "essential to the national interest." For fiscal 1985 he requested $1.1 billion for chemical weaponry, with binary nerve gas down for $105 million. (Protective garments for the military, in the amount of $431 million, appears in the fiscal 1985 budget.) And over the next five to seven years the Reagan plan is to spend $6.5 billion on chemical weaponry.* The fresh output will be added to our current inventory of 42,000 tons of poison gas—half mustard, half nerve. Dr. Robert Ruttman estimates that our stockpile of nerve gas contains 10^{13} lethal doses, enough to kill, several hundred times over, every human and animal on this planet. A July 1983 motion to ban production of chemical gases failed in the Senate 50 to 49; Vice-President Bush cast the tie-breaking vote.† The sum of $124 million was approved to begin production of binary nerve gas at Pine Bluff,‡ Arkansas. In November 1983, a House-Senate con-ference committee rejected the appropriation and in May 1984, the full House concurred, 247 to 179. But one can be confident that ways and means will be found to restore it.

The United States Army is considering the use of binary nerve gas shells as warheads on any ground-launched Cruise missiles that may be deployed in Western Europe during the late 1980s.

Twenty countries are believed to have stockpiled chemical weapons. As a consequence, defense against chemical attack has intensified. Over five years, the private Belgian firm Chemviron has doubled its sales of protective activated carbon. N. V. Seyntex, also Belgian, has roughly quadrupled its sales of protective material. Governments particularly interested include Denmark, Norway, Saudi Arabia, Thailand, and the

---

*So that, in any discussion of a worldwide ban on chemical weapons, we will "have something to bargain with."

†In November 1983, the Vice-President once again cast the deciding Senate vote, precipitating a conciliatory phone call from the President to the Vice-President's mother who had said, "I would die if this country would ever use it."

‡A job-starved city, in 1981 ranked by Rand McNally on quality of life 275th of 277 cities surveyed.

FOUR

Has the Bomb?

mb? Six nations, certainly. Shown with the year of first
osion they are:

1945
1949
1952
1960
1964
1974

ight nuclear power reactors. Among them are twin reactors
American-built (by General Electric) and American fi-
negligible interest rate). They are the main source of
r Bombay.

uclear power reactors can be made to yield 550 pounds of
annually, enough for 30 bombs per year. By 1985,* via its
essing plants, India may have 5,000 pounds of fissionable
nough to fuel a nuclear arsenal of world class. In fact, by

---

essing is not *already* underway, which in late 1984 is informed opinion. In
ium for India's 1974 fifteen-kiloton bomb, constructed in violation of the
nder which the Tarapur reactors were financed and built, probably was
m Tarapur spent fuel.

United States. The government of Sweden has already bought four
million gas masks, and is buying 400,000 new masks each year.

Germ warfare may find a place in the American arms program for
the 1990s. The release of bacteria, seventeen years ago, by the United
States Army into the New York City subway system, an act of which
the one million daily riders were not informed, revealed the practical
promise of pathogenic agents. The agent was *bacillus subtilis*, dangerous
only to the very old, the very young, and the very ill, but unfortunately
an agent readily carried by exposed healthy subway riders to such vulnerable populations. *Bacillus subtilis* survives for about 100 years.

Despite the fact that we are signatories to a 1972 treaty banning all
forms of biological warfare—a treaty signed by all major powers and
ninety other nations—the budget for biological weaponry under President Reagan is closing in on $100 million.

Deterrence by Nuclear Strength

*If there are no winners, then no rhetoric can disguise the
endless death upon which deterrence policy is based. Ask-
ing mere mortals to exercise perfect restraint while threat-
ening to destroy one another is more than an irony. It is
an irrational drive toward death.*

Chaplain Kermit Johnson,
Major General, United
States Army, retired.

The senselessness of a huge nuclear inventory for national
defense, the waste of billions of dollars needed elsewhere, the road to
global suicide widened by every new nuclear weapon—these would
seem to permit only one conclusion. In the United States, in the Soviet
Union, in every country on earth, nuclear arsenals must be destroyed.

But that verdict is not unanimous. There are many who believe that
the more nuclear weapons we have, the safer we are, that 20,000 nuclear
bombs are more protective than 2,000. Or than 50. That no one will
attack us, knowing that a totally destructive counterattack will follow.
While victory may be imaginable in war between countries with very
small nuclear inventories, victory is out of the question when nuclear
inventories are large; therefore, if no one can win, no one will try to
win. That our best course is to threaten what we want to prevent. That

47

since there is no practical likelihood of getting rid of *all* nuclear war-heads,* nuclear powers must learn to live and make policy in the midst of them. Finally, for thirty years it has worked.

This is a perilous method of preventing nuclear catastrophe, and it will be hard, particularly for young people, to accept it. Fifty thousand bombs. A continuous threat by two countries to destroy each other and much of the entire world, and the ever-available means to carry out that threat. And the means will become available not only to the Soviet Union and the United States but to scores of countries large and small, and to scores of leaders, rational or demented. Keep in mind that once forty nations have the bomb, and soon they will, other nations will—in fact will have to—intensify efforts to match them; in short, once forty nations, soon eighty. Also keep in mind that, if they are able to take ancient and powerful enemies with them, there is more than one nation on earth and more than one leader among them that might find the combination of international destruction and national suicide a thinkable prospect. George Kennan has written, "A nuclear explosion can serve no useful purpose. It cannot be used without bringing disaster upon everyone concerned." Doubtful comfort indeed. National disaster, like personal suicide, is always an option.

The more bombs we have, the more the Soviet Union fears us; what we call deterrence they call threat. And every new bomb we build (five each day) increases their fear. But every new bomb we build also in-creases danger to us. For the day may come when, irrationally or not, mounting Russian fear of us will suggest to them one last, desperate attempt at a solution—a first strike. And every word of this paragraph remains valid if USA and USSR are interchanged.

Deterrence, and the large inventory of nuclear weaponry that goes along with it, will have the support of the military, to whom more is always better than less. And the support of industry, for the bomb and all that goes with it is currently a sure path to large profit. And the support of topflight universities which, along with many of their science faculty, reap major financial benefit. But the cost to the rest of us will be high. In K. Subrahmanyam's words, a world of nuclear warheads

---

*In late 1983, former Secretary of Defense Robert McNamara said, ". . . the 40,000 nuclear warheads . . . are unlikely to be cut by more than 50% in the next ten, fifteen years. We're going to live for decades in a world of tension, and with tens of thousands of warheads, a few hundred of which can cause nuclear winter or destroy civilization."

"freezes permanen
over into every area
the people of the
hostage-holding nuc
to appear on the scer
of the military, an es
freedom. A world of
search for even better
ray from space, perhaps
perhaps all three. A we
risk of nuclear conflict
cident. And by madness.
earth life in a powder keg
are there. All that is need
this, and we can.

Who

Who has the bo
nuclear test exp

United States
Soviet Union
Great Britain
France
China
India

India

India has
at Tarapur,
nanced (at
electricity fo
India's n
plutonium
own repro
material,

*If repro
fact, pluton
agreement
extracted fr

1985 this figure may become 5,000 pounds *annually*; Tarapur alone will be able to reprocess 125 tons of spent fuel annually.

India is also constructing a fast breeder reactor, to be fueled by plutonium reprocessed from spent fuel of power reactors *not* at Tarapur.

In 1983 the United States was obliged to terminate its 1963–1993 nuclear export agreement with India,* not, however, before supplying India with 240 tons of enriched uranium. In 1983 France agreed to supply enriched uranium for the reactors—without insistence on peaceful use. The Reagan administration gave France its blessing and agreed to continue to supply needed spare parts.

In September 1983, despite all evidence to the contrary, Indira Gandhi announced that India had no nuclear weapons and had no plans to build nuclear weapons.

Three other nations have the bomb or could assemble one in a few months should they so choose. They are Israel, South Africa, and Pakistan.

Israel

The United Nations' 1982 inquiry concluded that "Israel reached the threshold of a nuclear-weapon state at least a decade ago." The CIA has confirmed that Israel was capable of building the bomb in the 1960s; major aid, in this early period, came from France and West Germany.† In 1974 the CIA reported that nuclear bombs had been assembled in Israel. In 1976, the CIA estimated 10 to 20 Israeli nuclear bombs. An independent report is more specific:

Israel possesses a nuclear arsenal of thirteen atomic bombs, assembled, stored, and ready to be dropped on enemy forces from specifically equipped Kfir and Phantom fighters or Jericho missiles.

In 1981 Egypt estimated the number of Israeli nuclear warheads at 27. Some Washington estimates are as high as 150.

---

*India refused to sign the 1978–1980 Nuclear Non-Proliferation Act. This act prohibits American nuclear exports to countries that do not permit IAEA to monitor their peaceful nuclear operations.

†Over the 20 years preceding 1976, 250 Israeli nuclear scientists were trained at the laboratories of the United States Atomic Energy Commission. To these must be added the substantial permanent migration of American scientists to Israel.

South Africa

South Africa has the bomb, or can have it when it so wishes. Beginning in 1982, South Africa's two new 900–1100 megawatt nuclear power reactors at Koeberg can yield 900 pounds of plutonium annually, enough for 50 nuclear bombs.

South Africa's raw uranium reserves are estimated at 300,000–530,000 tons. During the 1970s, Iran under the Shah was South Africa's leading uranium customer. Presently, with annual production of 6,000 tons (third largest in the world) from fourteen mines, South Africa's leading customers are West Germany, Japan, France, Spain, Taiwan (with a 3,400-ton contract), and the United States.

A South African bomb can be fueled either by plutonium obtained via reprocessing its own spent fuel or by enrichment, as soon as 1985 at its own facility at Valindaba, of raw to weapons-grade uranium. Or by purchase. South Africa recently bought 130 long tons of enriched uranium from the Swiss; the enriched fuel was converted to fuel rods in France.

An earlier source of weapons-grade nuclear fuel, sufficient for ten nuclear warheads, was 229 pounds of highly enriched uranium sold to South Africa by a friendly power, the United States. In 1976 this source was cut off by the White House and Congress, but the Reagan administration has found a way to restore supplies via Europe. The same friendly power also trained about 100 of South Africa's nuclear physicists and nuclear technicians.[*] In 1976, A. I. Roux, president of the South African Atomic Energy Board, stated:

We can ascribe our degree of advancement today in large measure to the training and assistance so willingly provided by the United States. . . .[†]

Over the years, in the area of nuclear warfare, South Africa's steady guide has been Israel. In fact, South Africa and Israel may jointly have

---

[*]About 80 nuclear technicians, now essential in the world of the bomb, were trained in the Atoms for Peace program, inaugurated by President Eisenhower in 1953. Sad to say, this program opened many doors to nuclear weapons proliferation. Over 150 American nuclear scientists have gone to South Africa, many on a consulting basis.

[†]Any current expression of gratitude would have to include West Germany, France, The Netherlands, England, and Israel.

exploded a nuclear device in September 1979. In return for its scientific aid, Israel has access to South Africa's uranium.

The government of South Africa considers the nuclear bomb to be an important adjunct to: (1) its long-run strategy to maintain apartheid, (2) its effort to prevent sanctions, and (3) intimidation of all African movements toward liberation and/or socialism.

Pakistan

If India builds the bomb, we will eat grass or leaves, even go hungry. But we will get one of our own.
Prime Minister Zulfikar Ali Bhutto, 1965

Pakistan is the extraordinary case. Here is a nation in need of but unable to pay for such basics as fertilizer and farm machinery. Yet within a year Pakistan will likely explode a home-built nuclear bomb. Financial support for this adventure comes from Libya and Saudi Arabia; the latter pours hundreds of millions of dollars into the Pakistani armament. *

Non-nuclear aid comes from the United States which recently guaranteed Pakistan a six-year grant of $3.2 billion for sophisticated arms. This grant could be suspended if the recipient explodes a nuclear device. But this is exactly Pakistan's intention. The Reagan administration sold Pakistan forty of our advanced F-16 fighter bombers (for $1.1 billion) to deflect Pakistan's request for advanced nuclear technology. In the end Pakistan will get both planes and bombs.

---

*Pakistan is one of Saudi Arabia's military outposts. But the latter hardly depends on Pakistan for defense. In 1982 Saudi Arabia bought more arms from the United States ($7.3 billion) than the United States sold to *all* countries in the previous year. Over the past eight years our arms sales to Saudi Arabia totalled $34 billion. These sales, which completely destabilize arms balance in the Mideast and which trigger equally high arms manufacture and purchase by Israel, are described by President Reagan as "an essential instrument of United States national security and foreign policy."

And not only sales to Saudi Arabia. According to the Congressional Research Service, from 1982 to 1983, our share of world arms sales to developing nations rose from 32% to 39% (the share of the Soviet Union fell from 27% to 17%, France from 18% to 5%). In 1982, President Reagan's first complete year in office, we sold $24 billion of war materiel, the highest figure by any one nation ever. In 1983, $21 billion. In 1984, we sold weaponry and provided military training to more than 100 nations.

Pakistan's eight new power reactors, upgraded to 900 megawatts, are under construction in the Chashma area, next to a reprocessing plant which by late 1984 should have been able to convert spent nuclear fuel into weapons-grade plutonium. Westinghouse is the reactor contractor, operating through legal loopholes provided by affiliates in Spain.* Nuclear hardware and technical advice come from France, Canada, Switzerland, West Germany, The Netherlands, and mainland China(!).† Uranium concentrate comes from Niger via Libya. At Kahuta, near Islamabad, is a uranium enrichment plant which probably became operational in early 1984; according to most accounts, it was built from blueprints stolen in The Netherlands. In short, all the ingredients for successful bomb-making are in place.

The Chashma plant is located on the Indus River, the only source of irrigation water for tens of millions of Pakistanis. It is near and possibly directly on a major fault in an area described by Columbia University experts as "highly seismic."

The people will remain hungry but: (1) Pakistani prestige in the Moslem world will rise, (2) Pakistan will now prepare, with greater confidence, for its fourth war with India, and (3) one more nation is added to the list of those that can destroy much of mankind.

Who Can Have the Bomb?

Who can, if they wish, build the bomb in one to three years? At least six countries:

Canada	Japan
Iran	Sweden
Italy	West Germany

---

*No American license will be needed. ENSA (Westinghouse) will bid, Nuclear Espanola (Westinghouse) will furnish design and software, SENER (Westinghouse) will build the reactor. When asked about this questionable arrangement, the Department of State, the Department of Energy and the Nuclear Regulatory Commission had no information. Westinghouse has eight foreign affiliates in the nuclear business, all outside American law.

†Ten orders of electrical material needed in uranium enrichment were successfully (and illegally) shipped from Canada; the eleventh shipment was intercepted. One shipment of zirconium, in the process of being smuggled out of the United States, was intercepted at Kennedy airport. How many were not? Pakistan uses a global network of foreign agents and dummy fronts (featuring agents in Turkey and fronts in West Germany and The Netherlands) to acquire whatever nuclear materials it needs.

And, if they wish, in four to six years? At least eight:

Argentina	Libya
Brazil	South Korea
Egypt	Switzerland
Iraq	Taiwan

And within ten years? At least twelve:

Australia	The Netherlands
Austria	Norway
Belgium	The Philippines
Denmark	Saudi Arabia
Finland	Spain
Mexico	Yugoslavia

Hans Grümm, deputy director of the International Atomic Energy Agency, has said, "Any really determined nation could now produce a bomb." Professor Daniel Yergin of Harvard has estimated 40 bomb-making nations by 1985. A more recent estimate by the United States Intelligence Survey is 31 countries by the year 2000. And the greater the spread of nuclear capability, the greater the risk that conventional arms wars will escalate into nuclear holocausts.

In the race for the bomb, four of the eight nations in the four-year to six-year category are moving forward with exceptional speed. Two are Brazil and Argentina, perhaps looking ahead to confrontation; the other two are South Korea and Taiwan.

Argentina

Argentina, with 1,200 nuclear scientists and technicians, over 230 of them United States trained, supported by high-level Swiss, Canadian, and West German technology, leads the nuclear race in Latin America. It is supported by the United States also; we sell equipment (recently a nuclear process control system) to the Swiss, who then sell it to Argentina. In 1983, at a cost of $100 million, much of it borrowed in the United States, Argentina obtained 143 tons of critically needed heavy water to moderate its nuclear reactors. It came from West Germany; it was produced in the United States. The shipment needed and got approval from the Reagan administration—a sharp policy reversal. (Earlier shipments of heavy water came from the Soviet Union.)

Argentina has a large store—about 50,000 tons—of natural uranium, and a commercial-size spent fuel reprocessing plant is under construction. Argentina will soon be able to produce substantial quantities of weapons-grade plutonium.

"Our electricity is the most costly ever produced," is a remark made by nuclear engineers in Argentina. But military nuclear potential is held to make the investment worthwhile.

Brazil

Brazil has 155 nuclear scientists trained in the United States, an uneconomic $30 billion investment in nuclear plants, and high-technology support largely from West Germany and Italy covering reactors, reprocessing, and uranium enrichment plants. The 1975 deal with West Germany alone cost $4.5 billion. A pilot reprocessing plant has been built, a breeder reactor is in process; there will soon be no problem with weapons-grade fuel. Moreover, a fourth nuclear center is being built—by the army.

All this despite a crushing national debt, to which nuclear weaponry makes a major contribution. But Brazil hopes to balance its huge nuclear (and oil) purchases by equally huge non-nuclear sales; 1983 military sales to thirty countries—with Iraq probably in first place—came to $1 billion. Already ranking sixth in the world, Brazil may move up; in October 1984, a new and wealthy customer—Saudi Arabia—signed a general five-year contract with Brazil.

South Korea

South Korea has committed $70 billion to construction, by the year 2000, of forty (!) nuclear power plants. Westinghouse (via its French affiliate Framatome), Lockheed, and French and Canadian firms are the principal suppliers. With only one clear enemy, a substantial proportion of this heavy investment is secretly directed toward the bomb; South Korea actively seeks a spent fuel reprocessing plant, either from the United States or France. With such a plant, South Korea can obtain 150 pounds of bomb-grade plutonium from each reactor.

South Korea is described by the CIA as a country "most likely and able to proliferate." And proliferation is promoted—by the United States in the form of loans for questionable power reactors. The American

Export-Import Bank (EXIM) has already committed $3.3 billion to South Korea's nuclear program.

Taiwan

Taiwan has six nuclear power reactors, built with the high-level technical assistance of Canada, Israel, and South Africa. Four are built on active volcano terrain, two on earthquake shock terrain. All were financed by EXIM. Taiwan's debt to EXIM had reached $2.2 billion by 1982. Taiwan will borrow $855 million from EXIM for two more reactors; the plan is for 24 reactors by the year 2000. Although Taiwan is one of the most densely populated countries in the world, there are no international safeguards on these dangerously located reactors.

By the late 1980s a simpler, less expensive method of extracting plutonium from spent fuel (see the footnote on page 59) will probably be available, and by the 1990s Taiwan will easily be able to produce 750 Hiroshima bombs. To what end?

All this on top of $800 million of non-nuclear military equipment annually from the United States.

EXIM

EXIM deserves mention here. While the Reagan administration speaks out against nuclear proliferation, EXIM finances, at lower-than-market interest rates, foreign purchases of reactors, some of which may produce more bombs than power. The bank's president states, "The EXIM bank has probably been the nuclear power export industry's best friend." True. Until early 1979 EXIM financed 47 reactors for 12 countries. The cost was $7.2 billion, with Westinghouse and General Electric getting $5 billion. And where does EXIM get its funds? From the United States Treasury, to which EXIM owes $16 billion. In America we have ceased to buy nuclear power reactors and we speak against the nuclear bomb. But we finance foreign nations to buy both.

Nuclear Scientists

Do these small nations have nuclear scientists to do the job for them? No problem. From 1955 to 1976, over 10,000 foreign nuclear scientists were trained in the United States. Hundreds have received degrees in nuclear physics from European universities. A 1981 estimate has Libya with 200 nuclear engineering students in the United States, 200 in Europe, and more than 200 in the Soviet Union. Pakistan has 550 nuclear physicists and nuclear engineers. The Stockholm International Peace Research Institute, as well as the distinguished Australian scientist Sir Mark Oliphant, estimate that one-half of the world's scientists are involved with nuclear or conventional weaponry.

Construction of the nuclear bomb no longer requires genius. A Princeton undergraduate, John Aristotle Phillips, designed a workable nuclear bomb: estimated cost—$2,000. Dmitri Rotow, a Harvard student (of economics), found full information for the construction of the complex hydrogen fusion bomb in the Library of Congress. Any reasonably capable physicist who spends a month in the library of the International Atomic Energy Agency in Vienna (or the MIT library) can return to his or her country ready to direct construction.

Uranium

Can the small nations buy uranium, even enriched uranium? As easily as Saturday Night Specials. An example is Libya's purchases from Niger. Niger ranks eighth in the world in unenriched uranium, now mining 4,000 metric tons annually (12,000 tons by 1986) at two multinationally owned mines in which the government of Niger has an important share. In 1981 Niger sold:

France	2,293 tons
Iraq	100 tons
Japan	817 tons
Libya*	1,212 tons
Spain	300 tons
West Germany	125 tons

These sales were accompanied by a statement from Colonel Seyni Kountche, president of Niger: "If the Devil asks me to sell him uranium today, I will sell it to him."

---

*The sale to Qaddafi in Libya is important. Up to 1979, 450 tons of Libyan-purchased uranium were undoubtedly transshipped to Pakistan and enriched there by facilities supplied by American and European firms.

A second example. In January 1983, Canada agreed to supply Canadian-mined uranium to the Philippines; the agreement included the customary assurance by the purchaser of "peaceful use." The contract is long-term, valued at over $1 billion. The fact that the Philippines ranks close to the bottom in human rights—Amnesty International has described scores of examples of torture, political persecution, and disappearance—played no role; any discussion of human rights abuses would, said (former) Prime Minister Trudeau, "be counterproductive to Canada's goal of increasing trade and commerce with the Philippines." Moreover, added the Prime Minister, "while human rights should be respected whenever possible, human rights and trade are not in the same league."

A small nation could reduce a major power to chaos with a half-dozen well-placed nuclear warheads. The fact that the instigator will within minutes suffer even greater chaos may be no deterrent. Irrationality is commonplace in national leadership. And there is no shortage of philosophies in which the ultimate sacrifice is not only admissible but admirable. At whatever cost to personal or national existence, bringing down the giants has long been an appealing idea. Now, for the first time, it is within reach.

Plutonium

Man-made plutonium makes better nuclear bombs. But where to get plutonium to fuel the new galaxy of American nuclear weapons? It is Reagan administration policy to encourage recovery of plutonium from the spent fuel of *commercial* reactors,* to reactivate the few dormant breeder reactors in the United States, and to support private and public construction of new ones; in the breeder reactor, plutonium is a major product. These steps, all of them rejected by President Carter, are ominous. Any increase in the supply of plutonium, particularly via privately owned plants, means that more plutonium will be lost, stolen,

---

*A forthcoming method of enriching uranium is known as laser isotope separation. It will be relatively simple and inexpensive. But, most important, it has one capability not enjoyed by (otherwise adequate) current methods of enrichment. It will retrieve plutonium locked in spent commercial fuel rods now stored in pools all over this country. These high-level waste pools may soon be regarded by the Pentagon as important assets, and the link between commercial nuclear power and nuclear bombs will tighten.

bought, sold, and used, and further proliferation of nuclear weaponry is assured. European and American public and private breeder-reactor programs will remove whatever slight lid still remains on the worldwide supply of plutonium.

And slight it is. In 1981 there were 500 commercial (and 340 research) nuclear power reactors operating or being built in 46 countries. Large commercial reactors average about 470 pounds of recoverable plutonium per year. This means a present annual worldwide total of about 240,000 pounds. At 18 pounds of plutonium (about the size of a grapefruit) to the bomb, a current annual total of 13,000 nuclear warheads is possible. In ten years the world can have 130,000 nuclear warheads, in twenty years 260,000. Other currently respected ten- and twenty-year estimates, assuming smaller bombs and more and larger reactors, are 167,000 to 592,000 warheads.

Here is an independent estimate: by 1985, the world's reactors will produce 47,000 metric tons of spent fuel rods, 30,000 tons of which will be in storage near the reactors. This waste can yield 175 metric tons of plutonium, enough for 21,000 bombs.

In the analysis of the Stockholm International Peace Research Institute, much larger numbers emerge. SIPRI estimates that by 1990 annual production of plutonium will be 900,000 pounds, permitting an annual construction of 50,000 bombs. Their estimate is 100,000 bombs per year by the year 2000. Senator John Glenn's estimate is even higher: assuming the use of plutonium from commercial power reactors alone, 200,000 nuclear bombs per year by the year 2000.

Dr. John Gofman, Director of Biology and Medicine at the Lawrence Radiation Center of the University of California, states that if two percent of the plutonium manufactured by the year 2000 reaches the environment, "assuredly, we can give up on the future of humans."

Plutonium and Uranium Lost and Stolen

Routine purchases and sales of plutonium and uranium are only part of the story. Thousands of pounds of plutonium and uranium—no one knows how many—are loose in the world today. Not only loose, but lost. American facilities operating under the supposedly strict supervision of the Nuclear Regulatory Commission and the Energy Research and Development Administration cannot find 3,400 pounds of plutonium and 4,800 pounds of enriched uranium. These have been lost in the thirty years preceding 1977 from twenty-five plants and laboratories located within the United States. This is enough to make 500 Hiroshima bombs.

Some has been lost during processing and is unrecoverable. But not all. In the single year ending July 1, 1976, 400 pounds of weapons-grade uranium and 120 pounds of plutonium were lost. The uranium included 200 pounds lost by manufacturers of submarine nuclear fuel. According to the Nuclear Regulatory Commission, at Apollo, Pennsylvania, over the period from 1968 to 1978, the firm of Babcock and Wilcox lost 438 pounds of uranium. Later in 1978 at the same site, another 25 pounds of weapons-grade uranium were "lost sight of." At the same site in 1965, 206 pounds of enriched uranium vanished; at that time Nuclear Materials and Equipment Corporation managed the facility. All signs—and these include recently released once-secret records of the Energy Research and Development Administration—point to Israel as the final repository of the 206 pounds.

Scripps-Howard obtained records indicating that between 1947 and 1982, a total of 1,700 pounds of highly enriched uranium was lost at the federal nuclear weapons plant at Oak Ridge. Security was tightened in 1979, but losses between 1979 and 1982 came to 178 pounds.

In one two-month period in 1979, at the processing operation run by Nuclear Fuel Services in Erwin, Tennessee, 20 to 48 pounds of bomb-grade uranium were lost or stolen. Published reports indicate that since 1957, up to 600 pounds of highly enriched uranium have been lost at Erwin.

In the first six months of 1981 the (Federal) Savannah River plant lost 35 pounds of plutonium. From October 1979 to March 1981, 25 pounds. Lost in the pipes? Accounting error? Stolen? No one knows. In 1968, with 200 tons of natural uranium ore on board, the *Scheersberg A* sailed from Antwerp to Genoa. It never reached Genoa. But it did turn up at a Turkish port, empty. The owner of the ship was an Israeli secret agent.

One millionth of one gram of plutonium, inhaled, will produce lung cancer. One pound of plutonium, properly distributed, is sufficient, over a period of twenty to thirty years, to kill every man, woman, and child on earth.

In a two-page advertisement taken in *The Wall Street Journal* by Dresser Industries, Professor Peter Beckman of the University of Colorado dismisses such extreme concern about plutonium: "A sheet of paper is sufficient to protect oneself from its radiation." This is true. If only the cells of our bodies were provided with sheets of paper to protect them from what we eat and breathe.

Nuclear War by Error or Accident

In 1975, 5,128 employees were removed from access to American nuclear weapons by the Personnel Reliability Program. In 1976 the number was 4,966, in 1977 the number was 4,973. Reasons: alcohol, drugs, "significant physical, mental, or character trait or aberrant behavior substantiated by competent medical authority." For aberrant behavior, 1,289 employees were removed in one year. Also 828 for negligence, 350 for court-martial or serious civil convictions. In the light of such figures, consider a published report by a former American missileer:

Four officers in a Minuteman squadron of fifty missiles can without any authorization begin World War III. If four men in two capsules turn their keys, no one could stop the launch.

Nuclear war by error cannot be ruled out. We have already noted the catastrophe that a Soviet computer error could produce if applied to Pershing II missiles (which travel at 6,000 miles per hour). At the North American Aerospace Defense Command (NORAD) inside Cheyenne Mountain in Colorado, in the eighteen months prior to October 1980, 151 false indications of immediate Soviet attack were recorded. Four resulted in a state of alert for B-52 bombers and intercontinental ballistic missiles, in preparation for retaliation. All errors were corrected in time but some were close. In June 1980, a 46¢ computer microchip failed; a Soviet nuclear attack appeared on the screen. Across the United States, one hundred B-52's, loaded with nuclear bombs, were on the runways. ICBM launch keys were in their slots; two turns and nuclear warheads would have been on their way—irretrievably. Twice in 1981, American Polaris submarines sent (correctly coded) messages that they had been sunk by enemy action. Fires in Siberian gas pipelines have been interpreted as incoming ICBMs; similarly, flights of migrating geese. On November 9, 1979, a technician ran, by error on live NORAD computer channels, a training tape showing a Soviet invasion of the

United States. Ten American fighters took to the air in six minutes, preparatory to a nuclear counterattack. Nuclear missile stations and nuclear submarines were switched to high alert. At the seventh minute the error was detected and the planes were called back.

The United States Navy currently deploys 600 nuclear missiles in 36 nuclear submarines. Each missile has 3 to 14 warheads; the destructive power of a single nuclear submarine is awesome. Note that the final decision to launch rests with *each* submarine commander, not with Washington; the risk of one irrational launch is not negligible. And not without risk are thousands of nuclear warheads, stored in 200 locations in 40 states, with security fairly easily breeched as repeatedly demonstrated by trained (American) teams. Nor is it reassuring to know that highly enriched (weapons-grade) uranium can be found on 23 American college campuses. In first place is the University of Missouri with 99 pounds, in second place MIT with 64 pounds. The risk of radiation is hardly slight. Nor is the risk of theft slight; highly enriched uranium sells on the black market at about $50,000 per pound. In all locations except one (University of Michigan), current college reactors require highly enriched fuel.

The Privately Owned Nuclear Bomb

In 1977 the Committee for Economic Development stated:

The engineering facilities required to design and build a plutonium bomb generally require no more than a building of modest size and the kind of equipment that can be freely obtained on the open market.

It may not be governments that drop the bomb. It may be adventurers, terrorists, or wealthy eccentrics. They would probably first buy, not build, a conventional nuclear power reactor; no fewer than fifteen countries* sell nuclear equipment on the open market. Now available are not only complete reactors and enriched uranium fuel, but reprocessing plants able to recover weapons-grade plutonium from spent reactor fuel. And, for a price, a nuclear trigger to ignite the bomb, or at least the design of a trigger. All this plus whatever technical support is needed,

---

*The United States has sold 59 power reactors abroad; West Germany, 40; France, 15. Canada appears ready to sell reactors (and uranium) to anyone.

as well as easy bypassing of the few international safeguards and the slight international supervision now in place. It is expensive. But for $250 million any group can acquire the means to blow up a substantial piece of the world.

Transport is unlikely to present a problem. If tons of illicit drugs can reach our shores monthly, so can a bomb. Nor will storage be a problem. The final product, the bomb itself, capable of killing millions and reducing to rubble, in seconds, any major urban area in the world, can be hidden under your bed.

Even tiny, inefficient nuclear bombs, readily constructed by amateurs, will serve the purpose of the terrorist. A one-fifth kiloton bomb, which could fit into a suitcase, would destroy the Empire State Building and everyone in it. Exploded near a reactor, it would bring death to thousands more. In fact, no bomb at all could be even more deadly. If the wind is right, a few pounds of powdered plutonium, attached to a commonplace explosive and dropped from a small plane, will produce a spectacular increase in the cancer death rate.

The CIA names fifty terrorist groups with 3,000 worldwide members. Between 1968 and 1980, 6,700 terrorist attacks occurred, one-third of them directed at U.S. citizens and U.S. institutions. Between 1970 and 1981 sixty-five nuclear attacks on the United States were threatened, at least four of them credible. *

The day of the private bomb will come, if in fact it is not already here. People will then not only live in fear of the Soviet Union, the United States, and forty other governments that cannot be trusted, but also in fear of scores of individuals and groups who can be trusted even less. And among these individuals and groups there may be some to whom the destruction of a part or all of civilized life would be the ultimate adventure.

---

*Other threats, several decidedly credible, involved nerve and mustard gas. Terrorists have easy access to a variety of toxins and chemicals, some of them equal to the bomb itself in ability to kill. To name one, ricin, 25,000 times as toxic as strychnine, is made from castor beans. Castor oil plants grow wild over much of the world; varieties are sometimes available at neighborhood nurseries.

FIVE
Unless . . .

National Leadership

National leadership has always chosen war as the final means of settling issues. From 1816 to 1965 there were 93 *major* wars among 144 nations. There have been 130 wars since World War II. There is no reason to expect anything different in the future. But there may be a different outcome. While two nations are "winning" or "losing" a war, the weaponry they finally employ may destroy both of them, as well as most of their neighbors.

But that fact may not deter them. Dr. Jerome Frank writes:

Humans faced with defeat always have resorted to the most powerful weapons they possessed. Under such circumstances, as Bertrand Russell put it, humans are more anxious to kill their enemies than to stay alive themselves.

There is no evidence that contemporary military leadership in any country understands the nuclear bomb to be anything more than a somewhat more powerful weapon than the TNT of World War II or the sixteen-inch shells of World War I. Discussing leadership by professional soldiers, E. P. Thompson calls them:

. . . a small group of military technicians, whose whole training and rationale is that of war, and who can, by no conceivable argument, be said to represent the rational interests of any economic or political formation. *

---

*It would be instructive to relate at length the eagerness of the late General Nathan Twining, United States Air Force Chief of Staff and later chairman of the Joint Chiefs

chological limitations on leadership in general, Dr.

logical obstacle to nuclear disarmament is the widespread
and peoples to grasp at an emotional level the magnitude
of the threat posed by nuclear weapons. . . . Only events that
have been actually experienced have a significant emotional impact. We re-
spond promptly to tiny environmental changes that impinge on our sense organs,
but readily ignore major aspects of the environment that do not. These include
nuclear weapons in distant countries poised for annihilation but which cannot
be tasted, smelled, seen, heard, or touched.

If you need evidence of how little international leadership has con-
tributed to the reduction of the stockpile of nuclear arms, note this
calculation by Sidney Lens: Since 1945 a total of six thousand nego-
tiating sessions have been held on disarmament; not one nuclear warhead, as a consequence, has been destroyed. In fact, quite the contrary.
From two small nuclear bombs in 1945, the world has progressed to
50,000 nuclear warheads with over a million times the destructive
power of the Hiroshima bomb. If we explode a mere one percent
of our current arsenal, the world could cease to exist as a livable
planet.

Do the awesome facts of nuclear destruction impress our leaders?
Not much. President Reagan dismissed European and American expressions of concern about nuclear weapons. These expressions, he said,
come from "increasingly vocal" groups, carrying a message of "pacifism
and neutrality." Former Secretary of State Alexander Haig has expressed
his willingness to fight a nuclear war. He also suggests that the United
States might underscore its resolve by a nuclear demonstration—in
Europe. Secretary of Defense Caspar Weinberger favors deployment of
the neutron bomb in Europe. He announced that the United States
will use nuclear weapons "if we have to." He is also considering nuclear
war "over a protracted period." The Defense Department report titled

---

of Staff, and General William Westmoreland, commander of American troops in Vietnam, to drop nuclear bombs on the enemy. To say nothing of the profundity that
accompanies eagerness. Here is General Twining's advice to the French in Indochina:
"You could take all day to drop a bomb, make sure you put it in the right place. No
opposition. And clean those Commies out of there and the band could play the 'Mar-
seillaise' and the French could march out."

Fiscal Year 1984–1988 Defense Guidance was revealed by *The New York Times* in May 1983. Here are two passages:

Combat against Soviet forces will be of higher intensity and longer duration, with weapons of much greater accuracy and possibly higher rates of fire and mobility. It will feature intensive electronic warfare and possibly chemical, biological, and nuclear weapons.

[American nuclear forces] must prevail and be able to force the Soviet Union to seek earliest termination of hostilities on terms favorable to the United States.

Harold Brown, Secretary of Defense in the Carter administration, said, "In our analysis and planning, we are necessarily giving greater attention to how a nuclear war would actually be fought . . . more stress on being able to employ strategic nuclear forces selectively." Eugene Rostow, former director of the Arms Control and Disarmament Agency, said, "We are living in a pre-war, not a post-war world." While speaking of "ten million (dead) on one side and one hundred million (dead) on the other," Dr. Rostow reminds us that this "is not the whole population." Also, nuclear weapons "permit us to use military force in defense of our interests with comparative freedom." Dr. Rostow's position was considered not sufficiently hawkish; he was fired by President Reagan.

Writing with Keith Payne, Colin Grey, foreign policy adviser to President Reagan and consultant to the Department of State, says, "the United States must possess the ability to wage nuclear war rationally." Moreover, American dead could be held to twenty million and that "should render the United States' strategic threat more credible." They add that:

Strategic forces do not exist solely for the purpose of deterring a Soviet nuclear threat. . . . Instead, they are intended to support a U.S. foreign policy. . . . Such a function requires American strategic forces that would enable a president to initiate strategic nuclear use for coercive, though politically defensive, purposes.

Consider President Carter's 1980 unpublished *Directive 59*, emphasizing nuclear targeting of Soviet troop concentrations, missile sites, and submarine pens, along with instructions to the Pentagon to prepare to fight (and win) a limited* nuclear war. *Directive 59* was supplemented by the appearance in 1981 of *Airland Battle 86*, which focuses on Europe and spells out *early* use of nuclear (and chemical) weapons in deep attack. This document states, "From the outset it is acknowledged that in this scenario it would be advantageous to use tactical nuclear and chemical weapons at an early stage and in enemy territory."

Finally, here is a 1980 interview, by Robert Scheer of *The Los Angeles Times* and author of *With Enough Shovels . . .* , which reveals the thinking of a man who may become President of the United States.

Robert Scheer:	Don't we reach a point with these strategic weapons where we can wipe each other out so many times and no one wants to use them or is willing to use them, that it really doesn't matter whether we're 10% or 2% lower or higher?
George Bush:	Yes, if you believe there is no such thing as a winner in a nuclear exchange, that argument makes little sense. I don't believe that.
Scheer:	How do you win in a nuclear exchange?
Bush:	You have survivability of command and control, survivability of industrial potential, protection of a percentage of your citizens, and you have a capability that inflicts more damage on the opposition than it can inflict on you. That's the way you can have a winner, and the Soviets' planning is based on the ugly concept of a winner in a nuclear exchange.
Scheer:	Do you mean like 5% would survive?
Bush:	More than that—if everybody fired everything he had, you'd have more than that survive.

Vice-President Bush's final estimate may be right. In an all-out nuclear war, the long-run percentage of "survivors" may be as low as 0% (Carl Sagan's estimate) or as high as 10%.

The views of our leaders translate into military policy and practice. A 1980 United States Army Field Manual states: "The U.S. Army must be prepared to fight and win when nuclear weapons are used." Action details are spelled out in literally dozens of Army, Air Force, and NATO

---

*"Limited" can often be interpreted to mean "limited to Europe."

field manuals. These manuals abound with phrases like "nuclear environment," "exploit the effects of nuclear fires," "offensive use of nuclear weapons accomplish objectives which would not otherwise be attainable."

Unless . . .

Silence in the face of inhumanity is equivalent to complicity.
Council of Jewish Federations

Dissent without civil disobedience is consent.
Henry David Thoreau

The perpetual threat and fact of national conflict cannot be permanently resolved without attention to causes. But some causes are historically well beyond the power of the best-intentioned modern men and women to resolve. History is replete with such; Arab-Jew differences have a two-thousand-year history. Beneath the customary cordiality of modern bargaining on lesser issues, deeply rooted antagonism remains.

Conflict has become commonplace. Moslems and Hindus, Moslems and Jews, Christians and Moslems, Catholics and Protestants, blacks and whites, communists and capitalists. But now, for the first time, waiting in the wings to serve *all* parties, is incredible nuclear armament, promising, even insuring, an instantaneous resolution of all differences. And a unique resolution—all parties destroyed.

It is the ever-present likelihood of nuclear war tomorrow—or today—that forces us to disregard causes, to be indifferent to the ways and means by which nuclear conflict can begin—"by accident, miscalculation, by the implacable upwards creep of weapons technology, or by a sudden hot flush of ideological passion," as E. P. Thompson writes. We must ignore the fact that social and economic inequities often lie at the root of nuclear threats. We do not have time to wait for education to civilize our world—the best but the slowest solution. We must seek a solution, at least a temporary one, before we even properly define the problem.

I propose two steps.

First Step: A Declaration by Each Nation

1. To agree to no-first-use of nuclear weapons.
2. To call a halt, at least a temporary halt, to current production of nuclear weapons.
3. To agree not to develop, manufacture, test, or deploy new nuclear weapons.
4. To destroy, over the first two years, 50% of all existing nuclear weapons, wherever stored or deployed, and to destroy 20% of the remainder each following year.
5. To take steps toward the conversion of nuclear weapons facilities and their workers to nonmilitary activity.
6. To give authority to the United Nations' International Atomic Energy Agency to monitor this agreement, and to meet regularly to settle details under this agreement.

Verification

There need not be major difficulty with verification. First, the historical record. Over the past twenty-one years the Soviet Union and the United States have reached fifteen arms agreements. Excepting the unratified 1974 Threshold Test Ban Treaty, the Soviet Union has carried out each agreement. President Reagan's 1984 revelation of five Soviet violations was followed by statements by Department of State officials who prepared the report—that none of the five alleged violations had military significance.* The United States Commissioner to the Standing Consultative Commission, which monitors compliance with SALT I, writes:

The Standing Consultative Commission has never yet had to deal with a case of real or apparent clear and substantial† noncompliance with an existing agreement.

---

*In October 1984, three weeks before the election, the White House announced 17 Soviet violations of arms agreements. One week later the Soviet Union announced "at least" 8 American violations.

†There is little point in minor violations; benefit does not match worldwide censure. The problem is to detect test violations that could decisively alter the balance of nuclear arms.

But reliance on the historical record is not needed. Objective verification of a nuclear warhead agreement is attainable, by surveillance satellites with cameras capable of photographing six-inch objects, seismographic technique, tamper-proof land cameras, and on-site inspection.

Space-based sensors can readily detect atmospheric tests of nuclear devices. For the more secretive underground tests, seismographic stations, of which there now exist about 1,000, can identify, locate and estimate the strength of a nuclear explosion. The detailed analysis of seismic verification technique in late 1982 by Sykes and Evernden concluded that a network of thirty seismic instruments, fifteen inside the Soviet Union and fifteen outside, could monitor a total test ban down to one-kiloton (non-earthquake) explosions.* Summing up, they write:

For many years the stated policy of the United States has emphasized the desirability of a complete test ban if verification could be ensured. The policy was not fundamentally altered by the recent decision of the Reagan administration to put off further negotiations on the test ban. On the contrary it was reported that the administration still supports the ultimate goal of a comprehensive ban on nuclear testing, but has doubts about the efficacy and reliability of seismic methods of verification. . . . There can be no substance to such doubts.

There is fear that one nation, say the Soviet Union, will develop a different and formidable nuclear weapon, one that will slip through the verification network and be deployed without our knowledge. This is entirely unlikely. Research, development, production, testing, and deployment require five to ten years. To evade detection over such a period would be impossible. Moreover, production of nuclear devices is possible at only three or four locations in any country; these locations can be readily monitored by satellites.

One reservation: It is true that the International Atomic Energy Agency, of which 115 countries are members, cannot at this writing reliably

---

*Lynn R. Sykes is Professor of Geological Sciences at Columbia University and a member of the delegation that negotiated the 1974 Threshold Test Ban Treaty. Jack F. Evernden is program manager at the United States Geological Survey's National Center for Earthquake Research. Their one-kiloton lower limit is certainly controversial; the correct figure may be closer to ten.

detect the diversion of reprocessed or enriched uranium to bomb use by on-site inspection or otherwise.

Job Conversion

From the viewpoint of jobs, conversion from military to civilian goods production can only be a gain. Many jobs have been lost by transfer of spendable income from the American people to the Pentagon. In a careful study by Employment Research Associates of the impact of the 1981 military budget ($154 billion) on industrial and commercial employment, the following job net losses and job net gains were revealed.

Agricultural Products and Processed Foods	85,000	jobs net loss
New Residential Building Construction	116,000	"
Lumber and Wood Products	70,000	"
Textiles and Clothing Manufacture	260,000	"
Newspapers, Periodicals, and Book Printing and Publishing	31,000	"
Motor Vehicles	206,000	"
Primary Metal Industries	35,000	"
Fabricated Metals	45,000	"
Transportation	15,000	"
Retail Trade	585,000	"
Wholesale Trade	66,000	"
Services	76,000	"
Banking, Insurance, and Real Estate	184,000	"
Ordnance and Guided Missiles	132,000	jobs net gain
Aircraft	189,000	"
Shipbuilding	40,000	"
Radio and Communication Equipment and Electronic Components	159,000	"

1,774,000 jobs lost, 520,000 jobs gained

To 1984, at least twenty-four public and private agencies have been studying job conversion to civilian production, and have been preparing detailed plans. The major proposed federal legislation are *HR425*, the Defense Economic Adjustment Act, introduced by Congressman Ted Weiss of New York, and *HR4805*, the Economic Conversion Act, introduced by Congressman Nicholas Mavroules of Massachusetts. The Weiss bill provides for (1) notification by the Pentagon of any cutbacks, (2) the creation of committees to deal with job conversion on lost or reduced military contracts, (3) interim income plus retraining for military production workers, (4) a federal council to coordinate job conversion plans, and (5) financial help for affected communities. The cost of *HR425* is estimated at one-tenth of one percent of the annual defense budget.

Second Step: To the Streets

If the leadership of any country fails to ratify the declaration, the people—adults and children—of that country must protest publicly; if necessary, in the streets. There is nothing else. Whether such behavior is described as democracy in action or civil disobedience or anarchy no longer matters. What matters is to achieve, by massive expression of will, a temporary worldwide assurance of survival as the critical first step toward the creation of a world in which people can live without fear of nuclear death.*

What form public protest will take, what we will actually do I cannot predict. But we must be prepared for the worst. Some—best the older among us—must be prepared to lose our freedom or even our lives so that billions of younger people can be assured theirs. There is nothing heroic or hysterical in this statement; it is an inevitable element of any final appeal.†

---

*Max Lerner, calmly reviewing Jonathan Schell's passionate *The Fate of the Earth*, informs us that "fear is a sterile force," and that we must act "without mass marches and parades, and without hysteria." Fear, mass marches, parades, and hysteria may be our final and only means. Facing the end of our lives and the end of all life, four billion of us may decide not to act quietly, or by proxy.

†A public uprising is the precise opposite of the solution offered in the Harvard Nuclear Study Group's *Living with Nuclear Weapons*, a book warmly received by the Reagan administration. Here warfare is viewed as a political game; the nuclear bomb merely enriches it. The common man stands on the sidelines awaiting his fate, hostage to a sophisticated political process of which he is hardly acknowledged to be a member. Even at the hour of his possible extinction, he is expected to remain a passive spectator. His fate, and the fate of the world, will rest on decisions made in high places, by the same coalition of academics, applied scientists and political leaders who got us into this situation in the first place. Moreover, the solution is no solution at all. Calm and thoughtful to the finish, the authors judiciously distribute plus and minus points to everything from weapons to ideas, ending up, as Andrew Kopkind writes, in "the empty center." Or, as Daniel Ford writes, "Quidem . . . autem—on the one hand . . . on the other hand." Kopkind describes the Harvard book well: ". . . a major effort to assert proprietary rights on the nuclear issue . . . aimed at the most worrisome alternative: a popular movement . . . define the debate in their own terms so that their university can have it . . ." Elitism may be a convoluted path to failure, but it gets there.

If our leaders fail, all that is left is ourselves. We must oppose those who believe that the situation is already hopeless, that self-destruction is inevitable now that the means are known or soon will be known by so many. We must not be frozen into inaction by the detailed horror of nuclear death. We must not be paralyzed by dehumanizing numbers and words—five million incinerated here, ten million asphyxiated there. We must not be numbed by the insanity of it all—a world that took four billion years to evolve coming to an end in one hour. We can no longer restrict ourselves to such weapons as indignation, incredulity, or anger. We can no longer delegate the elimination of this terrible threat solely to the governments that created it. Logical analysis, learned studies, fiery speeches, and books like this one have run their course. The spectre of nuclear annihilation is real and it is near. It will soon be one world or none.

Certainly no stone should be left unturned. In the United States, as many as 500 local and national organizations are struggling to bring an end to the threat of nuclear war. Of 185 Vermont towns, 161 voted in favor of a mutual freeze on the production, testing, and deployment of nuclear weapons. Sixteen state legislatures, 446 New England town meetings, 58 cities and towns, 320 city councils, and 71 county councils have voted in favor of bilateral or multilateral freeze proposals. In the general election of November 1982, voters in eight of nine states supported a nuclear freeze; the states were California, Massachusetts, Michigan, Montana, New Jersey, North Dakota, Oregon, and Rhode Island, with Arizona voting against. In the same election city support for a freeze included Washington, D.C., 70%; Chicago, 75%; Denver, 62%; New Haven, 72%; and Philadelphia, 76%. County support: Cook County, Illinois, 66%; Dade County, Florida, 58%; Suffolk County, New York, 69%.

One active organization is International Physicians for the Prevention of Nuclear War, with 100,000 members (not all physicians) in 53 countries. One of its two largest national affiliates is Physicians for Social Responsibility, with 19,500 American physicians in 149 chapters with, in recent years, a 1,000% annual growth rate. Much of this growth can be traced to the dynamic leadership of its former president, Dr. Helen Caldicott. The other is the Soviet Committee of Physicians for the Prevention of Nuclear War, with 20,000 physicians; in December 1982, 1,300 of its members gathered in Moscow for their first national convention.

74

In late 1983, 15,000 physicists, including many from the United States and the Soviet Union, signed an appeal to governments everywhere to end the nuclear arms race. An attempt to deliver the signed petition to President Reagan failed; he was too busy to receive the delegation. The President's science advisers also declined to receive the petition.

The current effort by zones, towns, counties, and cities to become nuclear-free—free of nuclear production, handling, testing, and deployment—deserves support. The movement began in February 1981 with Hawaii, the largest of the Hawaiian islands with a population of 92,000. The first area in mainland America to vote itself nuclear-free was Garrett Park, Maryland, population 2,800 in May 1982. By June 1983, the list included 23 areas. *

Public demonstrations opposing deployment of Cruise and Pershing II missiles in Europe, as well as production or deployment of *any* nuclear warheads *anywhere*, have been impressive. Here is an incomplete list through 1984. †

Public Demonstrations Against Nuclear Warheads

Amsterdam	400,000
Barcelona	75,000
Berne	30,000
Bonn	350,000 (50 special trains)
Brisbane	60,000
Brussels	200,000
Bucharest	100,000; 300,000

(list continued on next page)

---

*A 1983 drive to make Cambridge, Massachusetts nuclear-free failed; the vote was 17,300 to 11,700. The proposal would have halted existing research, testing, evaluation, production, maintenance, storage, transport and disposal of nuclear warheads or their components. Raytheon, Sperry, Avco, Draper (with $140 million in defense contracts) and other corporations poured $500,000 into a successful telephone and radio campaign. The presidents of Harvard and MIT (the latter school with $249,000,000 in military contracts—$50 million on campus, the remainder in nearby Lexington) found "constitutional flaws" in the proposal. A former president of MIT suggested that such legislation should originate at the Washington level; it appears that we should not carry the notion of grass-roots democracy too far. Professors, many working on Defense Department contracts, found the proposal vague, anti-intellectual, anti-research, a first step toward thought control. Nobel laureate George Wald of Harvard had no trouble finding the common denominator of this curious but successful coalition: money.

†President Reagan on American protesters: "Supporters of the nuclear freeze and peace movement are being manipulated by persons who want to weaken America."

Cologne	40,000
Comiso (Sicily)	80,000
Dortmund	125,000
Florence	200,000
Frankfurt	70,000
Gotheburg	100,000
Greenham (England)	30,000 (women)
The Hague	550,000
Hamburg	100,000; 200,000
Heilsbronn	30,000
London	200,000
Madrid	400,000
Melbourne	100,000
Milan	100,000
Moscow	800,000
Munich	20,000
Neu Ulm	50,000
New York City	750,000
Osaka	500,000
Ottawa	15,000
Paris	60,000; 25,000
Pasadena	80,000
Philadelphia	17,000
Rome	200,000
Stockholm	20,000
Stuttgart	100,000
Timisoara (Romania)	100,000
Tokyo	300,000 (at 3 rallies)
Vienna	70,000; 100,000
West Berlin	30,000; 50,000

During the week of October 15–22, 1983, three million demonstrated in West Germany. Approximately 220,000 formed a 67-mile human chain from Stuttgart to Neu Ulm.

A pastoral letter, condemning nuclear warfare in detail, was signed in May 1983 by 238 American Catholic Bishops; 9 were opposed. The letter originated in the Bishop's Committee on War and Peace, chaired by Joseph Cardinal Bernardin of the archdiocese of Chicago. This effort received strong (and somewhat unexpected) support in November 1983 from Pope John Paul II, who called on scientists to stop working on nuclear, in fact on all military research, to replace "laboratories of death" with "laboratories of life."

In May 1982 a Soviet-sponsored "World Conference of Religious Workers for Saving the Sacred Gift of Life from Nuclear Catastrophe" was held in Moscow. Nearly 600 religious delegates from 90 countries were present, representing Buddhists, Parsis, Hindus, Jews, Moslems, Sikhs, Shintoists, and Christians. A prominent participant was the American evangelist, Billy Graham.

A December 1982 United Nations resolution outlawing *all* nuclear explosions passed the General Assembly by 111 to 1; the negative vote was cast by the United States.

Continued negotiation among the great powers must be supported. The perennial and noble effort to abolish all war, nuclear or not, always deserves support; similarly, the decision by some feminists not to bear children until the nuclear threat is removed.

In every corner of the world there is some organized and much unorganized protest. But all of this may not be enough. A huge number of us may have to act, perhaps even violently. It is our world and it may be up to us to save it.

If we fail, we will all die. Not quite all. As so often, the leadership will survive. Where? Deep under a granite mountain, forty-seven miles west of Washington, with apartments, offices, ventilation, heat, medical facilities, electric subways, and a well-stocked cafeteria. With whom for companions above ground? Flies, mosquitoes, rats, earthworms, and cockroaches.

Acknowledgments

One

I am indebted to Dr. John Burke, head of the burn care unit at Massachusetts General Hospital, and to Dr. Howard Hiatt, former dean of Harvard's School of Public Health. I owe thanks to Dr. Herbert Abrams, head of radiology at Brigham and Women's Hospital, for research on unleashed diseases and to Dr. H. Jack Geiger, Logan Professor of Community Medicine at City College of New York, for his estimates of destruction in Omaha and elsewhere. Most of the material on Chicago originated in *The Progressive*, written by Erwin Knoll, editor, and Theodore A. Postol, physicist at the Argonne National Laboratory. Investigative reporters whose work has been of primary importance include Mary McGrory, Richard Severo, Michael Paul Roth, Robert Cooke, Melinda Beck, David C. Martin, and Marilyn Achiron. Also Chris Robinson and Kevin J. Kelley of the *Guardian* on the neutron bomb, and Robert C. Toth, Jack Anderson, and Takashi Oka on the same. I thank investigators Richard Burt, Ronald Koven, Angus Deming, Andrew Tolan, Edward Behr, and Christopher Ma for valuable information. I am indebted to Dr. Kathleen Adams for the sections on Montreal and shelters; on the latter, the detailed discussion by Peter Goodman, in *Nuclear War*, has been used. For material on San Francisco I thank Dr. Lincoln Fairley. Information and analysis have been published by Herbert Scoville, Jr., vice-chairman of the Arms Control Association, and by MIT Professor Henry W. Kendall, chairman of the board of the Union of Concerned Scientists. *Bulletin of the Atomic Scientists*, edited by Professor Bernard Feld of MIT, remains a critically important source of information. A variety of journals and newspapers have made original contributions; these include *Harvard Magazine*, *Time*, *The Boston Globe*, *Newsweek*, *Equal Times*, and *The Christian Science Monitor*. I have used estimates of human and property damage formed by Physicians for Social Responsibility and by Ruth Leger Sivard, the latter in *World Military and Social Expenditures 1982*.

The Physicians for Social Responsibility and the American Medical Association are leading sources of reliable information on medical effects; the former has been the vanguard in this effort. I have used the work of Dr. Victor Weisskopf of MIT on the impact of a twenty-megaton bomb on Boston, and of Dr. J. Carson Mark, former head of the Theoretical Physics Division at Los Alamos Scientific Laboratory, for similar judgments on one-megaton bombs. On the latter I also thank Jonathan A. Leonard for material that appeared in *Monthly Review*. I have borrowed material from Dr. Douglas Jacobs, from Dr. John Constable and Dr. Alexander Leaf, of Harvard Medical School, and, in quantity, from Dr. Helen Caldicott, former president of Physicians for Social Responsibility. I have borrowed from the incisive work of Dr. Kosta Tsipis, MIT physicist and associate director of the Program in Science and Technology for International Security. On Hiroshima the definitive source is *Hiroshima and Nagasaki; the Physical, Medical, and Social Effects of the Atomic Bombings*. Other sources are the work of Janet Bruin and Stephen Salaff in *The Progressive*, Kevin J. Kelley in the *Guardian*, and the journal *Awake*. I have used estimates by Jonathan Schell, from his moving *The Fate of the Earth*. I have used material from the Cato Institute Policy Analysis monograph by Arthur M. Katz and Sima R. Osdoby.

Two

Among the journals and newspapers from which I have borrowed are *The New England Journal of Medicine*, *The People*, *In These Times*, *The Nation*, *Newsweek*, and *The New York Times*. This section is particularly indebted to the American Medical Association, to NARMIC (National Action/Research in the Military-Industrial Complex), and, as always, to the Center for Defense Information. I thank Dr. Bernard Lown, Dr. Eric Shivian, Dr. Herbert Abrams, Will Reissner, William von Kaenel, and Dr. Henry Abraham. Also Dr. James Muller, who is a founder and officer of International Physicians for the Prevention of Nuclear War. Professor Bernard Feld and *Bulletin of the Atomic Scientists* have been the sources of valuable information. Also Spurgeon Keeny, Jr. and Wolfgang Panofsky in *The Boston Globe* and Rob Okun in *New Roots*. Investigative reporters who have uncovered valuable information include Steven Rosswurm, Richard Burt, and Mary McGrory. And, as always, Dr. Helen Caldicott. I have used Professor Henry Kimball's estimates on Europe, as published in *The Defense Monitor*. In this section and elsewhere, I have used material from Nigel Calder's *Nuclear Nightmares*. On shelters, I thank Jennifer Leaning and Langley Keyes, editors of *The Counterfeit Ark*. On long-term effects I thank Anne Ehrlich, Sharon Begley, John Carey, and Jeff Copeland. I thank Barbara S. Moffet and Fred Thompson.

Three

Investigators who have produced reliable stockpile data and judgments include Sidney Lens, Greg Speeter, Ted Greenwood, Carl Jacobsen, Professors George W. Rathjens and Jack Ruina. I have used basic data from the Stockholm International Peace Research Institute (Frank Barnaby, [then] director), and from the Center for Defense Information (Gene LaRocque, Rear Admiral USN [Ret.], director). Documented stockpile information has been repeatedly produced by *Time* and *Newsweek*. The annual *World Military and Social Expenditures* by Ruth Leger Sivard is invaluable. I have borrowed from the work of investigators George Church, Michael Schrage, Richard Halloran, Johanna McGreary, John Tagliabue, Brad Knickerbocker, Jack Reddin, Roberto Suro, Bob Levin, Fred Coleman, Merrill Sheils, Jack Colhoun, Arjun Makhijani, John Lindsay, Mary Lord, Martin Kasindorf, Strobe Talbott, Bruce Nelan, Kim Rogal, David Alpern, David C. Martin, Christopher Ma, and Howard Fineman. I thank Robert Aldridge and John Walcott. I am indebted to John Dillin of *The Christian Science Monitor* (and to the *Monitor* for other material), and to Kevin Kelley and Phil Reser, writing in the *Guardian*. I have used estimates by the National Academy of Sciences. I am heavily indebted to Randall Forsberg and the Institute for Defense and Disarmament Studies. Also, the Institute for Space and Security Studies, and Women's Action for Nuclear Disarmament (WAND). I thank Michael Klare.

For their investigative reports on space weaponry, I thank Charles Mohr, William Burrows, John Newhouse, Chris Woodward, John Noble Wilford, Robert Bowman, Edward Dolnick, Newell Mack, John Loretz, Philip M. Boffey, Michael Lerner, William Cook, Frederic Golden, John Tirman, William Broad, Jerry Hannifin, Congressman Ed Markey, and Bruce van Voorst. Also Curtis Peebles' *Battle for Space, The Boston Globe, The New York Times, The Washington Post, The Nation, Harper's, Newsweek, The Christian Science Monitor, Guardian,* and *Time.* For studies of MX, I am indebted to Fred Kaplan, Paul Warnke, Admiral Stansfield Turner, Gregg Easterbrook, Allen Sherr, Steven Roberts, Wayne Biddle, Robert Ruttman, and Leslie Gelb. Also *The Boston Globe, The New York Times, Defense Monitor,* and *Common Cause.* For incisive reporting on binary nerve gas and germ warfare, I am indebted to Jonathan Alter, Nicholas Horrock, David Rogers, Rick Atkinson, and Ben Bradlee, Jr. Also *The Washington Post, The Boston Globe, Newsweek, Science for the People,* The Union of Concerned Scientists, and Peace Priority. I have used information on and analysis of Cruise and Pershing II missiles developed by Anna Tomforde, Steven Erlanger, Martin Sheen, Drew Middleton, Charles

Mohr, and George C. Wilson. Again I must thank *The New York Times* and *The Washington Post*; also War Resisters League, Socialist Labor Party, *The People*, and *The Militant*.

Four

On Niger uranium I have borrowed information published by Anna De Cormis in the *Guardian* and by David K. Willis in *The Christian Science Monitor*; the latter's series of articles on proliferation have been path-breaking. I am indebted to Terence Smith of *The New York Times*. Also to Sharon Begley, Alexander Ha, Ross Allan, John Carey, Lynn Hall, John Bennett of Scripps-Howard, Frederic Golden, Melinda Beck, Christopher Ma, John Kohan, and Judith Miller. Among newspapers, *The Christian Science Monitor* and *The New York Times* stand out. I have used material first presented by David Burnham and David Binder in the *Times*, by Jonathan Harsch and John Yemma in the *Monitor*. I am indebted to Professors Joseph S. Nye, Jr. and Daniel Yergin of Harvard, and to Richard Strout. Also to Bob Levin and David C. Martin for their work on India. The investigative reporting in *Time* and *Newsweek* has often been excellent. I would also note the journal *Weekly People*. For facts and views on various countries mentioned in Part IV I thank Milton Benjamin, Andrew P. Hutton and Peter Ward. Also *The Lawrence Eagle-Tribune*, *The Boston Globe*, NARMIC, and *The Washington Post*. I am heavily indebted to the Center for Development Policy, particularly to Christopher Holmes, Lynette Peck, Katherine Dixon, Allison Noble, Linda Hunter, Virginia B. Foote, and Janine Holc. On Pakistan, William Beecher, *The New Republic*, and, for major analysis, *The Christian Science Monitor*. For important facts on proliferation, *The First Nuclear World War* by Patrick O'Heffernan, Amory and Hunter Lovins.

For detailed reporting on India, I thank William Claiborne and William J. Eaton. I thank *The Los Angeles Times*. For the same on South Africa, William Hartung, Frank Barnaby, *The Christian Science Monitor* (again with particular thanks to David K. Willis), SANE, and *World Press Review*. Valuable material on the freeze appeared in *The Nation* and in *Radical America*. For their work on nuclear power, I thank Manning Marable, Randall Forsberg, SANE, The Coalition for a New Foreign and Military Policy, and *Workers Viewpoint*. For valuable remarks on nuclear war by accident, Dr. James E. Muller, Jane Perlez, *The Defense Monitor*, *Newsweek*, and *The New York Times*. On shelters I have borrowed information and analysis from Bernard Feld, Andrew Tolan, SANE, and *Bulletin of the Atomic Scientists*. On campus reactors, I thank Kim McDonald and *Chronicle of Higher Education*, and for information on laser isotope separation, George Palmer, Dan Bolef, and *Bulletin of the Atomic Scientists*. I thank Christopher Raj, K. Subrahmanyam, and C. Raja Mohan, Paul Bracken, Alan Riding, and Lawrence Meyer.

Five

I am indebted to the *American Journal of Public Health*, and in particular to Dr. Jerome Frank. I have borrowed from the *New Left Review*, *The Nation*, *The Texas Observer*, *Bulletin of the Atomic Scientists*, NARMIC, and *Guardian*. I am deeply indebted to E. P. Thompson, Dan Smith, Joseph Rotblat, Jose Drucker, Norman Redington, Daniel Ellsberg, Doris Freeman, James Reston, and Nora Jennings. I have used material from *The New Abolitionist*, *Awake*, and *Nukespeak*, the last by Stephen Hilgartner, Richard C. Bell, and Rory O'Connor. My thanks to Roger Molander, Felicity Arbuthnot, Theo Brown, Derek Saunders, Fred Kaplan, John Somerville, and James L. Franklin. My thanks also to *Common Cause*, *Workers Viewpoint*, *The Boston Globe*, *Promoting Enduring Peace*, *Atlantic Monthly*, and *World Press Review*. For their work on conversion to peaceful enterprise, I am indebted to Professor Seymour Melman, Steve Early, Lloyd Duman, and Suzanne Gordon. I thank E. Barry Sheppard, William Gottlieb, *Socialist Labor Party*, and *The People*. For their contributions to verification, I thank Judith Miller, Mark Niedergang, The Institute for Defense and Disarmament Studies, SANE, and *The Christian Science Monitor*. I have borrowed from *Nuclear Peril* by Congressman Ed Markey, from *Arms Uncontrolled* by the Stockholm International Peace Research Institute (Frank Barnaby, Ronald Huisken), and from *The Arms Race and Arms Control* by the same institute. I thank Leslie Gelb and *The New York Times*, David Alpern, John Lindsay, Robert Cullen, Elizabeth Adams, and *Time*.

For corrections and improvements in all five parts, I am indebted to Dr. Bernard Feld of MIT, and to Admiral Gene LaRocque and Dr. Stan Norris of the Center for Defense Information.

To Dr. Kathleen Adams, of Columbia and Harvard Universities, thanks.

Index

84